Power, Politics, and
the Making of the Bible

Robert B. Coote
and Mary P. Coote

Power, Politics, and the Making of the Bible

An Introduction

FORTRESS PRESS   **Minneapolis**

POWER, POLITICS, AND THE MAKING OF THE BIBLE
An Introduction

Scripture quotations are translated from the original languages by the authors.

Cover design: Ned Skubic

Cover art: King Bar Rakab of Sam'al with his scribe. Used by permission of the Staatliche Museen zu Berlin.

Internal design: Karen Buck

Library of Congress Cataloging-in-Publication Data

Coote, Robert B., 1944-
    Power, politics, and the making of the Bible : an introduction /
Robert B. Coote and Mary P. Coote.
        p.   cm.
    Includes bibliographical references.
    ISBN 0-8006-2441-6 (alk. paper)
    1. Bible—History of Biblical events.   2. Bible—History of
contemporary events.   3. Religion and politics—History.
4. Sociology, Biblical.   I. Coote, Mary P., 1941-   . II. Title.
BS635.2.C66   1990
220.9'5—dc20   89-29954
                                                              CIP

The paper used in this publication meets the minimum requirements of American National Standard for Information Sciences—Permanence of Paper for Printed Library Materials, ANSI Z329.48–1984.   ∞™

Manufactured in the U.S.A.   AF 1–2441
94   93   92   91   90   1   2   3   4   5   6   7   8   9   10

A text without history
is a text which does not make history.*

*Pablo Richard, *La fuerza espiritual de la iglesia de los pobres* (San Jose, Costa Rica: D.E.I., 1987), 116.

Contents

Preface

This is a concise introduction to the Bible and how it came to be. It presents the making of the Bible as part of the larger history of the biblical period. It is meant primarily for those beginning their historical study of the Bible, but may serve as a review text as well.

It took a long time to make the Bible—in all, eighteen hundred years, roughly 1250 B.C.E. to 550 C.E.* The first date marks the appearance of Israel as a tribal power in Palestine, the second the legal definition of the Jewish and Christian organizations that instituted the Bible. Between these dates the Bible came into being.

Most readers of the Bible understandably find it hard to comprehend this long period, let alone fit what they know into a larger picture. This book supplies the picture, much like the cover on a puzzle box, or a map. It shows who did what, when, where, and why, and locates the Bible's main events and writings in their historical setting. Here you can discover quickly how the parts of the Bible were produced and how they interrelate.

This book says not the last word on its subject but a first. As a synthesis of a broad and complex subject, it is an invitation to further study, without which a little book makes little sense. It is the menu, not the meal.

Books have been written on the subject of nearly every sentence in this book. A concise introduction cannot begin to explain the ins and outs left unaddressed with every comma and period. The need

---

*B.C.E. ("Before the Common Era") and C.E. ("Common Era") are increasingly used as halfway attempts to find non–Christian substitutes for B.C. and A.D.

to forego detail and qualification has exasperated the authors at least as much as it may exasperate some readers. We only hope that not a few will be glad our finger rested on the delete key as often as it did. We have relied on the works of many, especially Chaney, McCarter, Corbett, Goodman, Neusner, and Williams. Works by these and others that have made a particular contribution to this book, acknowledged here rather than in footnotes, are included in the Selected Readings.

A relative chronology is located at the end of this work. We note here only that for the New Kingdom period the lowest chronology is followed, and for the monarchic period it is assumed that Hezekiah acceded after the fall of Samaria. Readers should refer to appropriate maps, such as those often found in Bibles.

The Bible began as the writings of a temple cult on the edge of the land bridge connecting Africa to Asia and the Indian Ocean to the Mediterranean. The history of how the Bible came to be tells how this cult began and lasted for a long time, and how its Jewish and Christian offshoots developed hemispheric significance. Given Palestine's strategic location, not surprisingly the temple's scriptures came to play a strategic role in a larger arena. Yet this development was not inevitable. The scriptures were nearly all written centuries before they assumed this role. Indeed, had it not been for the destruction of the temple by one Roman emperor and the support of its offshoots by others, these scriptures would probably now be of little interest.

The notion that the scriptures owe their enlarged role to their intrinsic nature contains some truth. Yet there was little out of the ordinary about the temple and its scriptures. This history explains how everyday people, circumstances, and events produced the Bible. Of course the Bible goes far beyond the mundane. Its sublimity, however, exceeds the scope of this book. The Bible is a source of endless amazement and inspiration, to which even an elementary historical understanding can make a contribution.

We thank the faculty of divinity of Glasgow University, George Newlands its dean, and the library of the university for their generosity and hospitality during the writing of this book, and particularly Robert Carroll and John Riches, heads of the Department of Biblical Studies during our most recent stay in Glasgow, for their patience and support, as well as Ernst Axel Knauf of the University of Heidelberg and Marshall Johnson of Fortress Press for their critical reading of this book in manuscript. Many others made critical comments and suggestions, for which we are grateful. We also thank Warren and Elizabeth Jacobs of the Royal Scottish Academy of Music and Drama in Glasgow for their kindness and assistance.

1

What Is the Bible?

The word *Bible* comes from the Latin form of a Greek word meaning documents. The Greek word is related to our word *paper,* though the Bible was around for a long time before it was ever written on paper. The Bible is a collection of documents. During the entire time the Bible was being formed, these were written by hand, on parchment (leather) and papyrus, mostly in scrolls.

The Bibles most people use are divided into two collections, the Old Testament and New Testament. These are Christian Bibles, containing the Christian scriptures. Originally the Old Testament was written in Hebrew (with some Aramaic) and the New Testament in Greek, both in forms of the languages not spoken today. A Bible in any other language, such as English or even modern Hebrew or Greek, is a translation, which offers the reader some plausible rendition of the original even when its meaning is not clear. In this book we usually call the Old Testament the Hebrew scriptures, since "Old Testament" is a Christian title and not all people who use the Hebrew scriptures are Christians. Many are Jewish.

The Jewish scriptures contain the same documents as the Protestant Old Testament (the Catholic Old Testament contains more), in addition to other writings. Jews call the Hebrew scriptures the Torah, Prophets, and Writings, or Tanak for short (after the first letters of Torah, Prophets, and Writings in Hebrew: *Torah, Nebiʾim,* and *Kethubim*). They also call them simply "Scripture" or, following Christian usage, the "Hebrew Bible." In addition to the Tanak, there are other Jewish scriptures. As Christians have the New Testament, Jews have the Mishnah, which developed into the Talmud. Although the Talmud is regarded as scripture, it is never printed or bound together with the Hebrew scriptures, nor is such a combination ever called the Bible. The relationship between the Hebrew scriptures on the one hand and the New Testament and Talmud on the other will be an important topic in the later chapters of this book.

As the Hebrew scriptures are equally authoritative for both Jews and Christians, the "Old Testament" cannot be equated with the Jewish scriptures nor the New Testament with the Christian scriptures. The Jewish and Christian faiths developed in relation to each other, between the first and sixth centuries C.E. (see note on page ix). Both faiths are based on the interpretation of the Hebrew scriptures, the one through the Mishnah and later Jewish writings, the other through the New Testament and later Christian writings. Indeed, it was through these two interpretations that the Hebrew scriptures eventually received their definition as the Old Testament or Tanak. The Hebrew scriptures are as Christian as they are Jewish, and the history of the Bible in the period after the fall of the temple in 70 C.E. deals with their interpretation in both organizations.

Jewish and Christian interpretations, alike in many respects, differed in the standard they used to interpret the Hebrew scriptures. For Jews the standard was oral law or torah (teaching), for Christians Jesus Christ, both with rather special definitions. Jews and Christians differed further in what they thought about the temple in Jerusalem and the legal significance of its scriptures. The Hebrew scriptures concerned social order, law, and the jurisdiction of the temple. Jews and Christians differed on what form the jurisdiction of the temple scriptures should take after the Roman destruction of the temple in 70 C.E. The Jewish interpretation stressed local jurisdiction, based on belief in the continuing holiness of the nation and its temple, even though the temple was no longer there. The Christian interpretation assumed imperial jurisdiction, based on the conviction that the temple and all it stood for had been replaced by the impending rule of God, which made Christians slow to define their own jurisdiction in the temple's place and ready to submit, whether happily or not, to Rome's jurisdiction in the interim.

These differences derived from the two main organizations that established their interpretations as authoritative. These were the Jewish patriarchate, or rabbis, and their schools and courts, and the Christian episcopate, or bishops, and their schools and churches. Scriptures were interpreted in and acquired their authority from the individual, organization, or institution to which they in return gave authority. Scripture meant not just writings, but writings whose authority some person or group maintained—usually against opposition. The history of scripture is a history of power, and of powerful organizations.

The Hebrew scriptures contain stories, histories, laws, prayers, hymns, predictions, proverbs, practical advice, theological reflections, love songs, official reports, and more. Its documents were mainly literary. The table of contents of an English Bible lists thirty-nine "books" of such material. Originally these were not separate books as we think of them, but scrolls. Often a composition was so long it had to be written on several scrolls. This was the case, for example, with the first four "books" of the Bible, Genesis, Exodus, Leviticus, and Numbers, which formed a single document or part thereof but were divided into four scrolls.

Sometimes several short documents were joined together to form a single scroll. This was the case with the twelve "books" from Hosea to Malachi, which are placed at the end of the Christian Old Testament due to Christian interest in prophecy pointing to Jesus Christ. These are sometimes called the "minor" prophets, only because they are shorter than the "major" prophets Isaiah, Jeremiah, and Ezekiel, not because they are less important.

Despite the variety of their contents, the Hebrew scriptures have one main subject—rulers of Jerusalem between 1000 and 150 B.C.E. and the people of Palestine under their rule. These people are variously called Israelites (Israelis are citizens of the modern state of Israel and played no role in the biblical period), Judeans, Jews, and, rarely, Hebrews, terms whose meaning will become clear. The Hebrew scriptures consist mainly of the scriptures of the temple cult of the god Yahweh in Jerusalem. The purpose of this cult was to legitimate rulers in Jerusalem, and this is what the scriptures are mostly about. Indeed, the writers of the scriptures became particularly active when rule changed hands and a new version of legitimacy had to be devised.

The initial purpose of the temple and its scriptures was to legitimate the ruling house of David (1000–520 B.C.E.) and after that the ruling priests established in David's name under Persian, Hellenistic, and Roman rule (520 B.C.E.–70 C.E.). After the destruction of the temple in 70 C.E., the purpose of these scriptures and their Jewish and Christian interpretations was to sanction the organizations that took the temple's place in preserving the scriptures.

The main subject of the Bible was thus rule in Jerusalem and else-where for the organizations preserving and promoting the scrip-tures, and the history of the biblical period is thus the history of rule. For this reason, and not from a failure to realize that history means more than politics, the history of the biblical period pays particular attention to rule. Since the history of rule was mainly the history of men's rule, this history is mainly a history of men.

The thirty-nine documents in the Hebrew scriptures are arranged differently in the Jewish and Christian versions of the Bible. The Jewish arrangement is closer to the original relationship of the scrolls. These arrangements began to develop even before there were codices, or books proper, to hold all the documents in a par-ticular order. The three groups of the Hebrew scriptures in Jewish usage—Torah, Prophets, Writings—contain twenty-four scrolls:

Torah
   Genesis, Exodus, Leviticus, Numbers, Deuteronomy
Prophets
   Joshua, Judges, Samuel, Kings (the "Former" prophets)
   Isaiah, Jeremiah, Ezekiel, Twelve Prophets (the "Latter" proph-
      ets)
Writings
   Psalms, Job, Proverbs (three "poetic" scrolls)
   Canticles, Ruth, Lamentations, Ecclesiastes, Esther (five festival
      scrolls)
   Daniel, Ezra with Nehemiah, Chronicles (more prophecy and
      history)

Samuel, Kings, Ezra with Nehemiah, and Chronicles were each divided into two in the Christian Bible, and in the Jewish scriptures much later, in the sixteenth century C.E., under Christian influence.

These three groups are of roughly equal length, but not of equal importance. The Torah was the most important. It contained the basic legal instruction and founding history of the nation Israel. (The concept of nation suggests a political consensus among the subjects ruled by Jerusalem; this rarely if ever existed, but the scribes who wrote the Bible worked for rulers who said it did.) The Torah legitimated the temple priesthood, the rulers of Jerusalem and its hinterland during the Persian, Hellenistic, and Roman periods—six hundred years. The Torah pictured the "nation" prior to its capture of Palestine, when Moses, who never set foot across the

Jordan, delivered its laws. It described the priestly cult of a later period as though it originated in this early time. Surprisingly, it mentions neither Jerusalem nor the temple, both essential to its centuries-long importance. This silence made it easier to find meaning in the Torah after the destruction of the temple. Some Judean groups later held that the Torah was the only scripture with real authority.

The Prophets were next in importance. The Former Prophets told the story of the nation and its rulers from the capture of its land under Joshua to the loss of the land under the house of David. The Latter Prophets addressed the legitimacy of the house of David and its temple, including the replacement temple established in David's name near the beginning of the Persian period, from several angles.

The Writings, while important in their own right, ranked below the first two groups. They contained various liturgical, reflective, historical, and prophetic documents. Unlike the Torah and Prophets, most of the Writings were composed after the fall of the house of David (about 520 B.C.E.). During the long period of the Torah's special authority, the Writings were a more open-ended collection than either the Torah or Prophets.

By the first century C.E., these twenty-four scrolls lay separate, to be joined together later into longer scrolls or codices. Yet the groups were already evident. The first four scrolls were a unity. The first nine scrolls, the Torah and Former Prophets, told a continuous story, from the beginning of history to the exile of the house of David. This group could not have been completed before 563 B.C.E., the approximate date of the last event referred to in them. The four scrolls of the Latter Prophets have similarities with each other, and all include texts that date to the period 550–450 B.C.E. Several of the Writings also come from this period, although some are later, and the latest of them, Daniel, was not written until 165 B.C.E. The last two scrolls—Ezra and Nehemiah and Chronicles—are related to each other, though their order is odd, since Chronicles looks like it should come before Ezra and Nehemiah. The Hebrew scriptures were thus essentially finished during the Persian period.

The fifth "book" of the Torah—Deuteronomy—originally formed the first scroll of the history contained in the Former Prophets. This history was composed in its present form toward the end of the rule of the Davidid kings. Not long after, in the Persian period, Deuteronomy was detached from the history and made the end of the fivefold Torah, when the scribes of the ruling priests conceived of the Torah as the whole law of Moses (with supporting history), including Moses' words in Deuteronomy. While Deuteronomy still kept its place "between" Numbers and Joshua, it changed its relationship to those two books.

Before delving into the history of the biblical period, it will be useful to form a preliminary idea of how the parts of the Bible relate to its main events. Here are some milestones to watch.

1250–1000 B.C.E.	Early Israel, before David
1000–970	David ruled Judah, then Israel
970–930	Solomon ruled, built first temple, established Davidic dynasty
930–722	Israel threw off the house of David, Jeroboam ruler of Israel; Israel existed as a separate kingdom
722	Fall of Israel
640–609	Josiah ruled Judah
598–587	Fall of Judah, Babylonian exile of house of David and temple priests, destruction of first temple
540–330	Persian rule; second temple built; restoration of ruling priests; end of house of David
330–152	Greek rule
152–63	Hasmonean (Maccabean) rule
63	Roman imperial rule began, continued seven hundred years
70 C.E.	Fall of Jerusalem, destruction of second temple
180–200	Mishnah; definition of New Testament began
313	Christianity became favored cult of Roman Empire under Emperor Constantine
380	Christianity became official cult of Empire; Palestinian Talmud written
428	Expulsion of Jewish patriarchate from Palestine; center of Jewish jurisdiction shifted to Persian Empire
530	Roman law codified under Justinian. Christian canon law and Babylonian Talmud written.

The Hebrew scriptures as we know them come basically from the Persian period (540–330 B.C.E.). Few were finished in the times they talk about (usually earlier than the Persian period), though they contain many texts, some long, written in earlier periods. The scriptures may be thought of as deep, complex palimpsests (manuscripts with one text written over another). In our view, with which many would differ, the kernel of each of the three main groups of scripture was a document written in the reign of David, near the beginning of the biblical period. For more than five hundred years the three groups as we now know them grew into being from their beginnings in David's court.

The Bible's earliest history, which historians call "J," embedded in a third of the Torah, was written in David's court to present the history of David's nation as David saw it. It explained how Judah and Israel were supposedly united against the threat of Egypt, David's arch opponent. A generation later, when people in Israel, led by Jeroboam, overthrew the house of David, the rebel court retained David's history of Israel but made many additions to it. These additions are called "E." Another major addition, of priestly traditions called "P," was added by a class of Jerusalem priests exiled to Babylon after the destruction of Solomon's temple and then reinfranchised under Persian rule. The result was the Tetrateuch, or first four books of the Bible, consisting of three overlapping justifications of rulers' cults composed for three rulers or ruling groups at the beginning of their rule, when each seized power from another (David, Jeroboam, priests: J, E, P). Later Deuteronomy joined to make the Pentateuch (Greek for "fivefold unit"), or Torah.

The Prophets grew in a similar way, starting with a document written in David's court demonstrating that he was innocent of the wrongdoing and impiety that seemed to accompany the overthrow of his predecessor Saul. This defense of David, after further additions regarding royal legitimacy from the courts of kings Jehu, Hezekiah, Josiah, and others, grew into the history contained in Deuteronomy through Kings (Deuteronomy and the Former Prophets), a lengthy legitimization of the long-standing house of David and its temple. Historians refer to this as the Deuteronomistic History.

The other prophetic scrolls, or Latter Prophets, consisted of expansions of original collections of speeches regarding the fall of Israel in 722 and of Jerusalem in 598 and 587. These also concerned the legitimacy of the house of David and its temple, and thus were associated with the great history on the same subject, even in its earlier stages.

The Writings were a cluster of documents dominated by the Psalms. The Psalms were the cult songs of the second temple, the one built during the Persian period and lasting six hundred years. The collection began, however, in the time of David and was used throughout the rule of the Davidic monarchy as well. The original core of the Psalms consisted of the prayers of David's private cult in his fortress Jerusalem.

The growth of the scriptures through supplementation resulted from the same process of interpretation often thought to apply only to the finished scriptures. Writing itself involved interpretation. As each new or revised writing was produced, it incorporated commentary not just on the writer's current situation, but also on the existing scriptures and their new meaning in a succession of current situations. Such variability led not only to new versions of old works, but varying texts of the "same" work. Some of these texts differed from each other considerably. In one case, Jeremiah was still being written when it existed in at least two versions, one a sixth longer than the other. This variability was also encouraged by the copying of the temple scriptures in distant places, like Egypt and Mesopotamia, in the Babylonian period and later.

The temple scriptures thus embodied a written tradition similar to other bodies of writings in the great cities of ancient Mesopotamia, Anatolia, and Egypt. The standard documentary tradition in Mesopotamia numbered over fifteen hundred clay tablets with cuneiform writing, all together containing much more text than the Hebrew scriptures. Palestine was small and poor compared to Mesopotamia. Clearly the Hebrew scriptures were not the earliest writings in the world, as was thought as recently as a century and a half ago, nor were they the only writings in Palestine in their time. Writing was widely used in cities by about 3000 B.C.E., though rarely for literature before about 2000 B.C.E. The Hebrew scriptures were written another thousand to two thousand years later than that. Moreover, in the biblical period much was written in Palestine besides the temple scriptures, but little is known about such writings.

The Judean "nation" in the Persian period was defined by Persian policy and authority. For hundreds of years thereafter, no significant change occurred in the pattern of imperial and priestly rule, nor in the temple scriptures. After about 400 B.C.E., the process of editing and adding to the existing scriptures slowed, although the ongoing modification of texts, still part of the process of interpretation, is well attested even in the sparse manuscript record. The scriptures were gradually translated into Greek, and ordered by subject and style: history, poetry, prophecy. This is the order followed in Christian Bibles.

New writings were produced, found today in collections called the Old Testament Apocrypha and Pseudepigrapha, which employed different methods of linking themselves to the corpus of temple scriptures. These methods included attributing the document to some famous person or writer in the scriptures, adopting the style or rhetoric of the scriptures, claiming special new revelation on a par with scriptural revelation, and salting the new work with explicit interpretations of scriptural texts.

In 70 C.E. the temple and its priesthood ceased to exist as such, causing a break in the process of scriptural interpretation in the service of the temple. Other organizations arose to take the temple's place in the lives of Judeans in Palestine and beyond. Within a century, it became clear that two surviving organizations were set to control the further interpretation of the scriptures: the Jewish rabbis and the Christian bishops. The rabbis produced the Mishnah and the two Talmuds based on it, the bishops the New Testament (as a collection) and the church's early creeds.

The Mishnah, the collection of writings of greatest authority for what became the strongest Jewish group, contained the legal pronouncements of several generations of rabbis, going back for over two hundred years, as these were remembered about 200 C.E. It consisted of tractates dealing with agriculture, feasts, marriage, court procedures, purity, and many other topics. The pronouncements of the rabbis were regarded as an oral Torah parallel to the written Torah of the scriptures and possessing equal authority. The Mishnah made only limited direct reference to the written Torah. In the light of the Mishnah, the written Torah of the scriptures was seen to be only one part of the complete two-part Torah. Subsequent Jewish interpretation, or midrash, showed the link between the oral Torah and the scriptures that the Mishnah itself made so little of. This interpretation was included in later works, culminating in the Babylonian Talmud of the sixth century.

The main organization behind the Mishnah was the rabbinic patriarchate, which descended from the school of Jamnia set up with Roman agreement after the fall of the temple. Later the center of rabbinic teaching and rule shifted to Galilee in northern Palestine. Under Rabbi Judah (170–220), the rabbinic head attained nearly royal powers in Palestine. The rabbis' governing role lasted until the Roman Emperor Constantine introduced Christianity as the favored Roman cult back into Palestine in about 330. By then rabbinic learning had spread to several schools in Persian Babylonia. When the Romans banned the patriarchate in Palestine in 428, the center of Jewish life transferred to Babylonia, where it remained for many centuries. Thus the paramount version of the Jewish scriptures today is the Babylonian Talmud.

The group that competed with the rabbis was the Christian bishops in the great port cities of the Roman Empire. They promoted a new set of scriptures that made their connection with the Hebrew scriptures more explicit than did the Mishnah. Thus the New Testament required less midrashic supplementation following its writing just before and after the fall of the temple.

The New Testament consists of twenty-seven works, most short. These include four narratives—one original and three based on it and other traditions—of the work, sayings, trial, and execution of Jesus Christ, called Gospels. The Gospels showed the connection between Jesus Christ and the destruction of the temple. This was a vital connection to explain, since before then the temple was as highly regarded among most Christians as among other Judean groups. One of the Gospels had a sequel, now called Acts, which carried on with the story of the movement founded by Jesus, as led by Peter, a disciple of Jesus, and Paul, a former rabbi turned disciple of Jesus Christ well after the latter's death. The Gospels and Acts make up three-fifths of the New Testament. The rest consists entirely of letters, twenty-one of them, with the sole exception of the concluding record of a revelation to a certain John. Letters were the common form of communication among the scattered Christian churches.

The two compilations, Mishnah and New Testament, are more similar than might at first be supposed. The New Testament was not regarded as a collection until about the time the Mishnah was compiled. Many traditions in the Mishnah are contemporaneous with the New Testament documents. The rabbis and bishops had quite similar histories for their first two hundred years. Accommodation with Roman power was essential to both, and both were tolerated by the Roman authorities. The standard of scriptural interpretation in the New Testament was Jesus Christ, who in this regard played a role comparable to that of the oral Torah of the Mishnah. The New Testament likewise follows its own organization and is written in Greek by authors not mentioned in scripture, thus like the Mishnah breaking the mold of the exclusive authority of the Hebrew scriptures. The forms of midrash, or interpretation, used by the Gospels, Paul, and the other New Testament writers were the same as those used in the Talmuds, from the exegesis of individual verses of scripture to the interpretation of themes through independent narrative.

The legal theme of the New Testament as a collection was stated in few places but implied throughout: the legitimacy of Roman jurisdiction. This contrasts with the emphasis of the Mishnah on detailing its own jurisdiction.

By the end of the second century, as the Mishnah was being compiled in Palestine, Christian teachers and bishops began to call the Hebrew scriptures the Old Testament, a phrase from one of Paul's letters (2 Cor. 3:4-17). The canon of Christian scriptures became defined as such under Constantine, the first emperor to favor the Christian churches, and his successors. There had been many other Christian writings, even some written earlier than those in the New Testament, but the New Testament contained the ones the imperial churches agreed to. The creeds of the churches were made necessary by the ambiguity of the Christian scriptures on certain issues where Christian philosophy and the relation of the churches to the empire were joined, especially the churches' understanding of monotheism, which was essential for the unity of the empire. The final definition of the legal spheres of empire and churches awaited the resolution of the issues set by the Council of Nicaea in 325 and the codification of Roman civil law in the sixth century, contemporaneous with the compilation of the Babylonian Talmud. By 550, the formation of the Bible, which had begun with the emergence of Israel eighteen hundred years earlier and to which this book serves as a preliminary guide, was complete.

The Bible was produced out of power struggles among rich men, as many down through the ages have recognized; thus rich men were its consumers and dominate its history. At the same time, more was going on and other kinds of people were involved. The next chapter gives an idea of what most people in Palestine were doing while a tiny few were producing the Bible. The majority had a lot to do with what went into the Bible, if not with its immediate production.

2
People of Palestine

The people among whom the Bible was created were just one of many groups living in Palestine at the eastern end of the Mediterranean Sea during the biblical period. As will become clear, they are to be distinguished from other people in the same area more by political than ethnic, cultural, or social criteria. Leaving aside historical developments for a moment, we can create a portrait of the lives of all the people who were the anonymous actors in eighteen hundred years of names, dates, reigns, battles, and documents, on the basis of evidence from the scriptures, other ancient texts, archaeological finds, sociological and ethnographic parallels, and descriptions of more recent times in Palestine.

Society as a whole throughout this period may be thought of as a hierarchy, or pyramid, with the greatest number of people at the base and the smallest number at the top. The pyramid was split into an upper and a lower section, the elite and the nonelite members of society. The elite were characterized by wealth—in the form of land ownership, power, and authority, lavish consumption of resources and a high standard of living, urban residence and cosmopolitan connections. They were rich. The nonelite, conversely, were poor, that is, comparatively landless and powerless, producers rather than consumers of resources, living at subsistence level in rural settings, their world limited mostly to family and village.

Among the rich, social stratification further split the upper section horizontally into numerous different elites, while political factions split them into rival vertical divisions. The lower section of the pyramid was less stratified horizontally, but divided vertically into overlapping affinity groups based on political, village, family, tribal, age, or gender ties, often extensions of elite factions. This pyramid of power was replicated at various levels throughout the society, from the peasant family with its patriarchal head, to the tribe with its chief or sheikh, the priesthood with its chief priests, and the royal court with its king. Each pyramid was bound together, up and down, by claims and responsibilities and by its common response to external threat, yet riven by internal struggles for greater shares of power and wealth and by the exercise and evasion of authority backed by force. Such factionalism created a tragic form of social order, whose oppression scarcely varied in intensity despite the changing strengths of successive central powers.

Position in the social pyramid was defined by relationship to the production of the grain that everyone, no matter how or where they spent their day, required for sustenance. While the many worked on the land growing the grain, the few generally kept and ate more of it. Most of the people of Palestine were occupied with raising wheat and barley to make their daily bread and to supply, directly or indirectly, the demands of their overlords. Wheat grew best in the broad arable of the coastal plain and alluvial lowland and highland valleys. Barley, having a shorter growing season, could grow in hills and more arid lands. Yields usually three to one and rarely more than five to one meant a nice and awful calculus weighing present consumption against future production, hunger against the need to reserve seed.

In addition to these annual crops, people cultivated perennials, chiefly olives and grapes, in orchards and vineyards. Olives, which thrive in the foothills and highlands, were raised for oil, consumed as the principal dietary complement to grain, and also used for fuel and ointment. Some kept livestock: sheep and goats for fiber for clothing, cattle for plowing, and asses for portage. Except among pastoralists, milk, with or without honey, entered the diet only as a last resort during seasonal shortages of grain, and meat infrequently, as the animals were more valuable to the villager alive than slaughtered.

People lived in patriarchal extended families, whose number and size were limited by the hardships endemic to life at the subsistence level: famine, disease, poverty. These bore especially hard upon children and women. If she survived to childbearing years (her chances were not so good as a boy child's), a woman might give birth to as many as five to eight children, spaced by postponing weaning, of whom only a few, if any, would survive early childhood.

Everyone in the family worked to contribute to the household economy. Some tasks would be divided into those for men (plowing and preparing land), women (preparing and storing food, drawing water, making clothes), and children (tending livestock); others would involve the whole family (hoeing, weeding, harvesting, threshing). Although the family, headed by a senior adult male, was a patriarchal unit in which male took precedence over female and age over youth, women were valued, all the more because they were relatively scarce, as essential contributors to the household economy, not only as mothers of sons. In the power pyramid of the household, the senior woman dominated the daughters and daughters-in-law. The patriarchal mystique also attributed to women a dangerous power for good or ill over the mysterious aspects of productivity and over life's major transitions—birth, death, and marriage. Patriarchy was a viable system not inherently cruel (whether or not it was unjust), which, however, under the strain of political and economic upheaval, could turn violent and oppressive.

Palestinian houses were built of materials available according to locality: sticks and branches, mud, mud bricks, thatch and straw, limestone, and occasionally wood beams. Some were simple one-room huts, some would have multiple rooms around a courtyard, others a second story (or more) or raised platform for family living, while animals were quartered in a courtyard or lower level. Houses were furnished with little other than a fireplace, matting for sleeping, storage bins and jars, and cooking utensils. Beyond the houses, some day laborers, poor nomads, outcasts, outlaws, misanthropes, and mentally ill people might live in caves in the countryside. While occupied with herding, some lived for more or less extended periods in grazing territory in tents, as did people looking after vineyards.

Houses were gathered in small clusters, villages, or towns, located in relative security, near a water supply, and sheltering usually from thirty to three hundred people, in rare instances up to a few thousand. Each village, isolated from other villages, could develop its peculiar ways of cultivation, depending on its ecological niche, its own customs in diet, clothing, and cult, its own variant of the local languages spoken in the region (one of the dialects of northern or southern Hebrew, of Ammonite, Moabite, or Edomite, or later of Aramaic), and its own ways to make music, dance, and stories.

Traditional religion in the village was bound up with agricultural production and family life, concerned with averting disaster and encouraging fertility. Spirits capable of bestowing or withholding benefits inhabited home, field, and well and required, like the authority figures in the political realm, to be tended and placated, or at least not provoked. People on the margins of household and village life, like childless widows or hermits, were regarded as having special power to mediate between ordinary mortals and preternatural forces, to induce prosperity or to cast the evil eye upon it. Some, as local holy people, saints, heroes, or "prophets" (in this book "saint" will be used for such figures in all periods, to indicate the similar role behind the several titles), gained enough prestige beyond the single village to assert their authority in broader contexts, speaking on behalf of a wider community to challenge or legitimate the exercise of power. Their tombs were venerated, and tradition recounted the return of many from the dead—though many more of the deeply mourned never returned. Worship took place in household and local village shrines and numinous spots, like the saints' tombs. Festivals celebrated turning points in the agricultural year and in the life cycle of the family. Villagers knew of the gods and goddesses of the religion of the cities and royal court but had little to do with official cults and their written traditions. Like all cult ceremonial, their observances were a hopeful investment of resources in social order, with better or worse results.

Working on the land, as most people did, meant having some kind of right to the use of the land concomitant with some kind of responsibility to an authority higher up. These relationships ranged from outright ownership of land to slave labor on someone else's land. A villager might be a cultivating small owner, a cultivator paying fixed rent in cash or kind, a cultivating head of a work team, a sharecropper possessing some productive aids like an ox or ass, a sharecropper with only labor to sell but with a regular position on a work team or attached to a parcel of land, a worker with a regular wage paid in cash or kind, a part-time seasonal worker, an indentured servant (debt slave), a slave at forced labor (corvée or statute labor), or a simple slave. Few villagers actually owned their land. We shall see as this history progresses how much of the Bible is concerned with the downward slide of farming families to the bottom of this scale.

All arable land belonging to a particular village was subject to periodic redistribution among the families holding cultivating rights to it. Thus a block of a half or a third of the village land would be left fallow each year and bounded for grazing. This practice, besides allowing the soil to recover fertility through resting and manuring, rotated the advantage of farming better land among families rather than leaving it an inherited right. It also meant that the village paid taxes as a community, not as individuals, through the village headman who represented the village in the outside world. The land cultivated in a given year could also be grazed, by the flocks brought in from winter grazing to feed on the harvest stubble in late spring.

The use of land was subject to heavy exactions from the state, the tribe, large landowners, and creditors. Claims from above on those below consisted chiefly of taxation in kind, which could take over half a cultivator's yield. Other taxes and dues were paid in labor, cultivating, harvesting, building, and fighting for overlords and the state. Where the rural economy was commercialized, taxes might be paid in coin. Creditors, to whom villagers struggling to wrest a living from the land often fell prey, would take land if the defaulting debtor had any, usually grain-producing arable that large owners preferred to turn to more profitable perennial crops for trade. Otherwise they would enforce the labor of the debtor or a member of his family. Anticipating the loss of the bulk of their crop to tax collectors and creditors, the laborers on the land had little incentive to produce more than what they required for subsistence, while those with an interest in large yields in grain and in tradable commodities like wine and oil knew little or nothing about farming and had no way except conquest to enlarge production.

In their relationships with their superiors, villagers were dependent upon patrons at various levels of authority: village headmen, credit brokers, landlords' factors and stewards, large landowners, local lords, tribal chiefs, and kings. These patrons were their only defense, by no means a reliable one, in legal and credit disputes and conflicts over resources. In return, besides yielding them their land and labor, villagers would be recruited to support their patrons in factional strife and warfare. Their life was a balance between submission to incessant demands from above and resistance to them by evading and cheating on claims, withholding produce and labor, or in extreme circumstances abandoning cultivation altogether for mercenary hire, banditry, or pastoral nomadism.

Some of the rich, such as the more prosperous villagers who could hire workers to cultivate their land and owned tools to rent out, or the officers of absentee landlords, lived among the villagers, but most were town and city dwellers. They came from many regional, ethnic, and linguistic backgrounds and spoke twenty or so languages over the biblical period, including the Palestinian dialects already mentioned, Egyptian, Hittite, Hurrian, Luwian, Greek, Phoenician, Aramaic, Assyrian, Babylonian, Persian, Latin, and Arabic. Their life was generally more comfortable than that of the villagers: they ate more and better food, including quantities of meat, they wore finer clothes and lived in larger and better houses, and, barring the perils of accident and war, lived longer, healthier lives. It was not, however, an easy life.

Like villagers, the rich lived in household groups dominated by the senior adult male. Buttressed by his cult, the head of the household ruled over his dependents, clients, and lands as a tax collector, magistrate, and military commander against whom there was virtually no appeal. Adjudication as practiced by such magistrates was essentially a contest of power, subject only to confirmation by cult, local spirits, and saints, the last being conduits for the flow of power to balance the claims and charges of contenders powerful and powerless.

Wealthy households were political, rather than simply domestic, units that included all sorts of non-kin retainers in the service of the head. The household's main business was maximizing its intake and possession of resources, that is, taking the produce and labor of the village, while villagers saw their best interests in minimizing their output beyond essential needs for survival. In the struggle to enlarge its control over more productive land and producing population, a household would be constantly engaged in forming alliances with some powers while fighting with others. Violent conflict was their primary occupation. Anxiety about inheritance and succession intensified at the top of the political pyramid, but concern for the integrity of private property was shared by all owners.

The cults of the rich, like those of the village, were intimately concerned with their daily occupations, warfare and conquest, and the administration of resources. Urban and state cults worshiped named gods with well-defined functions, such as Baal, the divine warrior, family founder and head, bestower of favorable weather and productivity of the land, and defender of the established order of society; his goddess consorts Anath and Astarte; and El, chief of chiefs, a dweller in tents on the paths of trade and travel through tribal lands; and his consort Asherah. Others in the pantheon included Horon, patron of the underworld home of fallen fighters; Reshep, the protector of fighters; and Shamash, the sun, light of true judgment. These cults, articulating and legitimating the power of their devotees, required ostentatious consumption of meat, luxurious clothes, fine utensils, precious metals, and jewels. The cults were housed in magnificent buildings, commissioned by the powerful to be built by the labor of the poor, and practiced elaborate rituals and prayer services.

Most significant for understanding the Bible, the cults of the rich and powerful had the skill of writing and produced scriptures intended to legitimate the institutions of state and temple. Because these scriptures, like their strong and wealthy sponsors, made protection of the poor in theory an essential platform, declaring God's option for the poor, they could be turned against the rulers or institutions that commissioned them, or read with profit after their demise. As a result of such reversals, bouncing the scriptures from rulers to ruled, we have the Bible.

3

Israel Before
the Bible

Palestine lies on a crossroads of trade routes running by land and sea through the Fertile Crescent of the Middle East—the Tigris and Euphrates valleys, the Mediterranean, and the Nile Valley. Empires rising in North Africa, Mesopotamia, Asia Minor, and Europe have contested its territory over the centuries. Its history is one of domination by a succession of imperial powers and is recorded in its early stages only in the monuments, tablets, and papyri of great powers with a story to tell. What we know as Israel was formed among the peoples of Palestine during Egyptian occupation of the New Kingdom era (1550–1150 B.C.E.) and defined itself in the contest between the Egyptian and Hittite empires, joined later by European invaders, over Palestinian territory.

Prior to the New Kingdom era, Palestine of the Middle Bronze Age had been thickly settled in fortified, prosperous urban sites enjoying high agricultural production. The total population may have been close to 150,000 people, or two Super Bowl crowds. About 1550 the Egyptian elite overthrew their alien overlords, the Hyksos from Palestine, and under a new dynasty embarked on an expansion of trade and power. Where New Kingdom Egypt came into conflict with the Hittites from Anatolia in the eastern Mediterranean, Palestine became a frontier and buffer between the two empires. According to some estimates, its population fell to as little as half its former numbers, and productivity declined.

In the fifteenth century, the pharaoh Tuthmose III made himself the feudal overlord of most of the coastal lowlands of Palestine. Besides plundering Palestinian cities and carrying away captives (including hostages from the leading families), military equipment, precious objects, grain, and livestock, the Egyptian conquerors required annual tribute in agricultural produce, as well as other provisions, corvée labor, and military service. They established a network of garrison cities in Palestine that also served as depots for the grain and provisions going to support Egyptian power at home and abroad. Palestine and the south central coast became an administrative district under the name Canaan, a term that referred generally to the inhabited areas of Palestine plus the southern coast of Lebanon. In the cities, Palestinian authorities were replaced by or subordinated to Egyptian officials, who worked through loyal local strongmen or warlords (sometimes known as "kings," a word that normally but not always designated autonomous sovereignty) to collect grain and provisions, protect trade, and administer the occupied territory.

The Amarna letters uncovered a century ago near the Nile, a collection of letters from foreign kings and Egyptian vassals to the foreign office in the Egyptian capital, reveal the nature of Egyptian imperial control during the reigns of Amenhotep III and Amenhotep IV (Akhnaton) in the first half of the fourteenth century. Rather than imposing a uniform regime, the Egyptian governors dealt with their Palestinian subsidiaries individually, pursuing a policy of divide and rule. Every town was hostile to every other. Conflict among local warlords, unless it threatened Egyptian authority, served Egyptian long-term interests. Especially on the margins of occupied Palestine, like the central hills, local strongmen could attain relative independence as long as they paid up the tribute on demand.

In the late fourteenth century, renewed conflict with the Hittites brought Egyptian campaigns back to Palestine. The reigns of Rameses II (1279–1212), Merenptah (1212–1202), and Rameses III (1183–1152) saw the greatest intensification of New Kingdom Egyptian power in Palestine. When after an evenly fought but decisive battle in 1274 Egypt halted the further advance of the Hittites, Palestine enjoyed a lull in hostilities for half a century. Garrisons were strengthened, collection of provisions became more stringent, great building projects were undertaken, and, under Merenptah, attempts were made to extend Egyptian rule into the central and southern hill country. Palestine was subject to Egyptian palace law and direct Egyptian taxes. Architecture, art, ritual, and cult were influenced by Egyptian practices. But the same period saw as well the beginning of the collapse of Egyptian power in Palestine.

Settlement patterns in Palestine under Egyptian occupation reflected the constant economic and political upheaval. Aside from the urban centers under Egyptian control, the typical settlement was a small town, of rarely more than a thousand inhabitants, with its associated villages and hamlets. Insecurity and oppression drove many people out of agriculture into pastoralism or banditry. Much of the land was left uncultivated. As another avenue of evading the pressures of occupation, after 1200 B.C.E. agriculture and villages began to spread in the north central highlands into areas that had not been settled for five hundred years or more, and to sites that in many cases had never before been occupied.

Egyptian scribes describing the conquest and administration of Palestine frequently mentioned dealings with groups called *apiru* or *abiru*, possibly the source of the term "Hebrew." As the rare uses of "Hebrew" in the Hebrew scriptures indicate, these appear to have been people displaced by the perpetual economic hardship and warfare, migrants of no one ethnic identity. They were usually, though not always, villagers or sedentary tribal folk driven by war, famine, debt, taxes, and military conscription to abandoning their customary occupations in cultivating the land. These unemployed tended to form mercenary fighting squads and engage in banditry and gang fighting. Many entered service to the highest bidder among the urban or tribal leaders requiring supporters whose military skills and loyalty could be bought, unhampered by kinship ties. Gangs were fluid entities, forming and disintegrating as members joined and later married and settled down to urban life under the protection of their lords. Derogatory use of *abiru* as the equivalent of renegade resulted when scribes described the use of gangs against established authority.

What and where was Israel in Egyptian-occupied Palestine? Israel was a name for power, the power of a tribe or confederation of tribes formed in the New Kingdom period in relation to Egyptian authority. The name itself, "El commands (the tribal forces)," which incorporates the name of El, the tribal chief among the gods, reflects the tribal nature of this power. A tribe was a political network of families united by external threat, claiming descent from a putative forebear, but not necessarily actually related as kin. Tribal identity competed with other loyalties to the state, class, and faction, in the constant contests for power. Though tribal ideology could be egalitarian, in practice the tribe, like other social structures, was a pyramid topped by the chief or sheikh, who was military commander, magistrate, and administrator of land and resources for dependent tribal members. The tribal hierarchy paralleled that of the state and could both compete and collaborate with it.

The first written reference to "Israel"—the only reference outside the Bible before the ninth century B.C.E.—also implies tribal identity. A stela commemorating a campaign supposedly undertaken by the pharaoh Merenptah in 1207 B.C.E. (it may actually refer instead to the depiction in reliefs at Karnak of a campaign of Rameses II) records:

> Israel is stripped bare, wholly lacking seed,
> Hurru has become a widow, due to Egypt.
> All lands are together at "peace":
> Anyone who stirs is cut down
> By the king of Upper and Lower Egypt, Merenptah.

"Israel" here is accompanied by a hieroglyphic sign indicating a tribal military force, not a city or town. Evidence suggests it was located in the north, in the buffer zone between Egypt and the Hittites. It could well have served as one of the arms of Egyptian administration in that area. The names of early leaders that survive in Israel's tradition are Egyptian: Moses, Aaron, Phineas. These figures may have been among the indigenous leaders taken to Egypt for training and returned to govern for Egypt in Palestine.

The chance for Israel's chiefs to emerge as a dominant force in the history of Palestine came about with the fall of first Hittite and then Egyptian power in Palestine. The overthrow of the Hittite Empire by one of the "sea peoples," as the Egyptians named them, Aegean or European invaders known as Ahhiyawa (possibly Homer's Achaeans), began while Rameses II still ruled Egypt. Pressure from these European forces in the west allowed Assyria at the same time to advance against the Hittites from the east. Under a similar threat from European sea rovers and land raiders, Egypt's policy at this time was to foster good relations with the Hittites and also to allow its client Israelite chiefs to extend from their northern frontier base into the central highlands, where they sponsored or took over much of the new settlement occurring there.

A generation later, during and after the reign of Rameses III, another group of Europeans, known as Philistines (hence the name

Palestine), established themselves in Egyptian-held parts of Palestine and gradually took over as Egypt's administrators and mercenaries. Building up their power in five base cities, Gaza, Ashkelon, Ashdod, Gath, and Ekron, they became settled in the south coastal plain, low foothills, and before long the rest of the lowlands, and by the third quarter of the twelfth century evicted the Egyptians altogether. The withdrawal of the two empires from the scene left it open for a contest between two erstwhile Egyptian proxy powers, the Philistine military oligarchy settled in the coast and lowlands and Israel's paramilitary tribal chiefs settled in the highlands, both rapidly expanding their power.

Israel developed into a highland power on an expanding agricultural base, therefore, as a result of three changes in the circumstances of empires competing in Palestine: the fall of the Hittite empire, the Philistine takeover of the Egyptian positions in Palestine, and the withdrawal of Egypt. A brief release from imperial pincers allowed the tribal confederation of Israel to expand its settlements from the northern lowlands and frontier to the central highlands and assert itself as a political power.

With various peoples settling in the highlands at various times during the twelfth and eleventh centuries, the population there grew from about twenty thousand in the mid-twelfth century to twice that many a century later. The settlers did not constitute a distinct ethnic or national group, and were never organized in a uniform and permanent pattern of tribal relationships. As an alliance of tribal heads, early "Israel" was little more than a constantly changing political entity. Nor was there an orderly migration of coherent named tribes into defined territories. Settlement in the highlands, in what was to be the heart of the kingdom of Israel, came first to the area later (and perhaps also earlier) called Manasseh, already partially occupied, then to Ephraim, Benjamin, and later in the eleventh century Judah.

The Israelites, or clients of the chiefs of Israel, continued as they had in the northern frontier lands to maintain themselves by village agriculture. Settled in small isolated villages, they cultivated arable fields for grain, tended orchards, and raised some livestock. Sites of this period, not exclusively Israelite, are characterized by use of a pillared house plan, decentralized production and storage of grain, storage pits, and a limited range of utilitarian pottery styles. Production of grain for the moment was locally controlled, subject only to the exactions of the tribal rather than urban elite. Israelite cult and jurisdiction were probably likewise decentralized, dispersed among local authorities. Tribal chiefs and priests promoted the cult of El under the epithet of Yahweh, "Producer," or "Pouncer," whose veneration was soon to become established through the state cults of monarchic Israel. This name referred to El as the originator of the tribal fighting and raiding host, the numerous and stalwart sons born to the growing highland populace. Tribal affairs were conducted at regional shrines, including Shiloh in the Ephraimite hills and Bethel in the Benjaminite hills. There the chiefs' struggle against the European lords of the lowland was organized and touted as the justification for the chiefs' continued tribal rule.

4

David Begins
the Bible

With imperial competitors temporarily withdrawn, the two local powers took up the fight over the Palestinian bone. By the mid-eleventh century the Philistines, organized in a warlord confederacy of palace cities on the coast and lowlands, had consolidated their hold in the former Egyptian strongholds and were campaigning into the hills to seize trade routes, subdue tribal forces, and take over tribal lands and workers. Responding to this threat in the north and central highlands, the sheikhs of Israel tightened their traditional tribal form of rule, allowing the hierarchy to become more sharply defined. Before long encroaching Philistine urban rule was met by Israel's tribal monarchy.

Late in the eleventh century a chief from the tribe of Benjamin, Saul, claimed the royal prerogative as chief commander of Israelite forces to assign fiefs of land to his supporters and to levy taxes. He may not have been the first king of Israel, as Asian warlords working for Egypt had used that title and tribes were often sufficiently integrated with urban rule to produce dynasties and kings, as suggested by the stories of Gideon and Abimelek (Judges 8–9). Saul is the first known, because of the role he was to play in the history of the usurping house of David.

Saul nearly succeeded in driving the Philistines and their allies from the highland watershed and upper Jordan Valley back to the coast. But the Philistines united to crush him, and Saul and three of his four sons perished in battle. What remained of Palestine not yet under Philistine control now fell into two parts. In the north, the surviving son of Saul, Ishbaal, whose name suggests a connection with the cults of Baal, took command of Israel, supported by Saul's cousin and commander Abner. Newly settled Judah in the south fell to David, a younger son in a large family from Bethlehem fathered by Jesse.

David had begun his ambitious rise in Saul's service and married Saul's daughter Michal. Looking to his own advancement, he was dismissed for insubordination. He relocated to the wilderness to the south and east of Judah and gathered an outlaw band of mercenary troops under his command. Apparently lacking support in his own family, except for some nephews, his sister's sons, whom he used and later discarded, and thus unhampered by kinship ties, David built his power by marrying into powerful and wealthy families. Although he temporarily lost Michal in his conflict with Saul, after Saul's defeat, from which he was conveniently absent, he acquired Saul's wife Ahinoam, who bore his first son. By then he had established marriage ties with the Calebites, the leading family of Hebron, by arranging the death of his own brother-in-law, a Calebite, and marrying the widow, his sister Abigail, thus becoming a wealthy landowner.

Aside from his marriages, David derived support mainly from Israel's enemy, the Philistines. In return for leading his gang for Philistine overlords in campaigns against desert tribes like the Amalekites, he received Ziklag south of Gath as a fief, a plentiful source of provisions and a base for handing out his own fiefs to his troops. Before long he became a quasi-tribal sheikh on the dryland border, with an urban base and control over extensive marginal and uncultivated lands and their flocks, as well as trade routes to the southwest and southeast. On his return to the hills with a large and eclectic troop that included Philistines and other European hired fighters, he captured Hebron and declared himself king of Judah. He then moved against Ishbaal to claim Saul's Israel. Linked to Saul's household by his alliance with the now-deceased Jonathan, Saul's son, and by reunion with Michal, David profited from the murders of Abner and Ishbaal to become king of Israel, though publicly he condemned the assassinations. Later he captured Jerusalem, a fortress town controlling an important route between coast and Jordan Valley, and moved his capital there, to the border between his united kingdoms. From this position he proceeded to overthrow rulers in all directions and create his own Asian empire. Thus, using Philistine forces, David, the one-time Philistine vassal, was able to fulfill for Israel the Philistine dream of controlling nearly all Palestine from the Red Sea to the northern Bika Valley in Lebanon. His next task was to co-opt the support of the tribes, to avert the hostility they were bound to feel toward one who had risen through the lowland network.

Except among his own gang, David was never popular, but he earned a measure of tolerance from his subjects thanks to his practical restraint in government and skillful public relations. (David's son Solomon, despite his reputation, was not nearly so clever.) David maintained royal rule over the tribal highlands by allowing tribal jurisdiction to take its traditional course in that area and by rewarding his supporters and palace staff with the yield of his external conquests rather than granting fiefs in Israelite territory. Lighter taxes were laid on the Israelite villagers than on conquered peoples. He achieved tenuous security on his borders through alliances, for example with the Phoenician coastal city Tyre, and by placing garrisons in strategic localities. He also settled Levites, a tribe of priests fiercely loyal to tribal ideals, with domicile and pasture rights but no permanent landholdings, in towns and villages on the frontier and lowlands and in Saul's former domain in Benjamin. He buttressed his throne with propaganda, promoting his success and the legitimacy of his rule in literature and ritual.

This one-man show could hardly last. Opposition to David's rule even at home came during his lifetime from defeated rivals in the families of Saul and Caleb, and from his own sons, most notoriously Abishalom (Absalom). His successor Solomon proved unable to retain the whole of David's realm and enforced such tyranny on the tribes that the next king lost all but Judah, where, however, the descendants of David (at least nominally) ruled for another four hundred years.

In David's realm, the traditional patterns of tribal jurisdiction prevailed in most aspects of highland life, while state jurisdiction on the Egyptian model, possibly learned from the Philistines, was superimposed where necessary to maintain royal authority, such as in requisitioning corvée labor (under the minister of labor, Adoram) to build the fortifications for Jerusalem. Parallel hierarchies, tribal and state, functioned in military and cult administration. Although the tribal militia was maintained under the command of David's nephew Joab, David's personal guard and troop of Europeans (Cerethites and Pelethites: Cretans and Aegeans), commanded by his crony Benaiah from the extreme south of Judah, formed the real heart of Israel's military force. In the cult, Abiathar of the house of Eli presided over the vestiges of the tribal cult of Shiloh and the tribal mobile battle palladium, the chest (ark) of Yahweh, and probably supervised the scattered Levite cults. Zadok, the reputed founder of the long-standing priestly line attached to the Davidic dynasty, ruled David's house cult in Jerusalem, which was probably conducted, at least at first, in a tent shrine in deference to tribal custom, as well as David's pilgrimage cult in the Sinai, on the border with Egypt. The state god to whom David's cult was devoted was Yahweh (translated LORD in many English versions), the Israelite manifestation of the warrior El as the chief god of the confederated tribes. (Yahweh was also referred to as El and, using an honorific plural, as Elohim, both usually translated God.) Benaiah and Zadok, the army and the cult, represented the twin bulwarks of David's throne and of Solomon's in the next generation.

Literature from David's court formed the germ of what became the Hebrew scriptures. It was not produced for popular consumption, literacy being limited to a few wealthy and the scribes in wealthy employ, but to appeal to the powerful few whose support David needed. Only a tiny fraction of David's subjects knew or cared what it said.

In chapter 1 we saw that each of the three groups of documents in the Hebrew scriptures—Torah (cult history and law), Prophets (court apologetic; defenses of and challenges to rule), Writings (prayers, sayings, miscellaneous)—began its life in the scriptorium of David's court and cult. Furthermore, David's usurpation of Saul's rule and quest for legitimation was the first in the long chain of changes in rule from David to Constantine that generated the Hebrew scriptures and their official Jewish and Christian interpretations.

The first requirement of royal propaganda was an apologia, or justification of David's actions in establishing his rule. Accordingly David commissioned the kernel of the Prophets, an account of his overthrow of the house of Saul, which appears in 1 Samuel 15 to 2 Samuel 5, asserting David's loyalty to Saul and acquitting him of any implication in the deaths of Saul, Ishbaal, or Abner. David's success is attributed solely to the solicitude of Yahweh. Further to allay suspicion among Saul's supporters among the Israelite sheikhs, what became 2 Samuel 21:1-14 and 2 Samuel 9 demonstrated the purity of David's motives—he was only acting on divine command—

in executing seven members of the house of Saul. The account in 2 Samuel 13–20 is addressed to Judahite supporters of Abishalom, depicting the rebellion as a private affair, an individual adventure that caused David much personal grief. The ark narrative in 1 Samuel 4–6 and 2 Samuel 6 tells how Yahweh himself returned the lost palladium through awesome powers to Israel and then allowed the dangerous object to be carried safely into David's city. Other shorter documents preserved include a list of the top fighters in David's early band, in 2 Samuel 23. Moreover, scribes could already draw on an earlier collection of fighters' poetry with a royal bias, the "Document of Yashar" (Josh. 10:13, 2 Sam. 1:18).

To legitimate his rule in broader terms, David, like any winner in historical conflict, needed a general history of his subjects that would show the inevitability of his success. This became the kernel of the later Torah. A large portion of Genesis and Exodus and some of Numbers, known as J (its writer is sometimes called the Yahwist), was composed as a history of early Israel from the creation of the world and its human inhabitants through the creation of Israel. Based in the literary tradition of Mesopotamia familiar to David's scribes, creation stories were appropriated to put Israel in a universal framework on a par with great powers like Egypt. The history was also designed to appeal for the loyalty of tribal sheikhs in the Negeb and Sinai, David's buttress against Egypt in the south, by suggesting that Israel's early chiefs, the patriarchs, were southern sheikhs like themselves rather than northern highland or presettlement sheikhs. Furthermore in the story Abram, introduced into Israel's tradition as its ancestor, must migrate from the east to facilitate a transition from Mesopotamian stories of early humanity to early Israelite history. Another new ancestor, Isaac, is pictured at peace with the Philistines: Egypt is the common enemy, contrary to what an Israelite might have continued to believe, given Egypt's earlier tie to Israel's chiefs and Egypt's support of Israel as the struggle against the Philistines developed.

David's scribe used tribal nomenclature and copied David's twelve-tribe structure of administration in order to foster the integration of tribes like Judah with Israel. History was reversed so that some historical latecomers to the highland conglomerate, members crucial to expansion of David's rule, like Simeon and Judah, were made older than Joseph and Benjamin, the representatives of heartland Israel. Manasseh and Ephraim, representing the territories settled first and the heartland of potential opposition to Davidic rule, were even placed in the following generation, mere sons of Joseph. All the tribal brothers, however, were reconciled to one another, in particular Judah and Joseph through the deference of Judah, in united opposition to the "national" enemy, Egypt. Egypt, on the brink of further adventurism in Palestine, was the principal enemy of David's Israel, now that his kingdom had been consolidated with the help of Philistines. So Egypt became the villain of the history, even though Israel in fact took form under Egyptian aegis.

Thus the formative event in David's history of Israel was escape from corvée labor for Egypt in the Delta, the main theme of the book of Exodus, not from the real threat to its heartland from the Philistines, with whom Israel had long contended, to say nothing of the threat from the likes of David himself. Moses, the putative forebear of David's supporters the Levites, though in reality possibly a Palestinian in Egyptian administration, was linked with a traditional story of south Palestinian pastoral nomads and Hijazi Midianites and his authority made absolute, as by implication David's should be. Moses' name is given to the author of David's law, which was limited to the rules of David's cult, focused on an earthen altar and featuring the traditional harvest festivals of barley, wheat, and dry-season fruits. The conclusion of the history was that any attempt to subvert the sacral legitimation of David's rule and its blessings, endorsed by vassal kings, was an outrage against none other than the divine creator.

This history also includes reflections of pre-Davidic eleventh-century compositions, shaped by their placement in the J document. Examples include Miriam's victory song in Exodus 15, Israel's blessing of his tribal sons in Genesis 49, and four blessings of Israel by a non-Israelite mantic named Balaam in Numbers 23–24. Similar to Miriam's song and possibly older, the song of Deborah in Judges 5, celebrating a tribal victory over urban forces out of Hazor in northern Palestine, indicates a pattern of women's victory song in Israelite tradition.

The Writings portion of scripture began with the liturgy of David's private cult, the official cult of the state conducted for David and his family and court alone. This consisted of sung prayers to Yahweh modeled on traditional prayer to the divine patron of unjustly accused and persecuted individuals, itself patterned on patron-client relations in the village. Retained as the basis of address to Yahweh in the royal court, these petitions, including most of the psalms in

Psalms 3–71 with the heading ". . . of David," harked back to David's wilderness years, when he and his outlaw gang protested others' unjust exercise of power. Most of David's subjects probably never knew how their king's prayers resonated with the grinding experience of their daily lives.

5
Solomon and the Temple

Solomon, born tenth in line to inherit the throne from David, jumped the queue, outmaneuvering Adonijah, the eldest surviving son and the tribal choice, and his other half-brothers to take the throne on David's death. Young Solomon was promoted by David's ministers Zadok and Benaiah and the court's pet oracle Nathan, and by Solomon's mother Bathsheba, queen of the harem, along with David's palace guard under Benaiah. This palace coup completed the takeover of Israel by the Negeb and European forces wielded by David. Solomon's rule was the creation of four old men left from David's reign—Benaiah, Zadok, Nathan, and Adoram—who elevated him and wrote his scripts.

With Solomon succeeding Saul and David, however, an apparent pattern for establishing royal authority over Israel was set: a legitimating saint (Samuel for David and possibly Saul, Nathan for Solomon) should anoint the new king, the king should set his capital in a new city (Jerusalem), and should establish a cult under royal patronage, and he should sponsor the writing of new or adapted scriptures to tell the new winner's history.

Solomon's kingdom sat across two major trade routes linking the Middle East and the Mediterranean. The coast road ran north from Egypt along the coast to Megiddo in the Jezreel Valley, then branched west to Akko, Tyre, Sidon, and more distant ports on the coast, and east to Hazor, Damascus, and thence north to the Euphrates Valley. A land route, the King's Road, connected with routes from Arabia and the Red Sea and went north through the hills and plateaus east of the Jordan to Damascus, where it merged with the coast road. Great wealth passed on these routes through Solomon's realm, and arms traffic, in the form of horses and chariots, too. Eastern Mediterranean trade in Solomon's time was dominated by the Phoenician (the Greek term) or Canaanite (the Egyptian term, in Solomon's time usually called "Sidonian") maritime kingdoms, the foremost among them being Tyre. Egypt also was returning to the Palestinian scene, at first nibbling at Solomon's western border and later in control again of the whole Philistine plain. On the north loomed the Aramean kingdom of Syria with its capital at the crossroads of Damascus.

Solomon fostered good relations with his powerful neighbors by cultivating trade networks of alien merchants, including allowing the practice of trading partners' cults in his realm, and making valuable marriage alliances. His marriage to an Egyptian princess, a first in Israelite diplomacy, was publicized, though there is reason to doubt the Egyptian crown in fact broke its rule against such marriages. The neighbors, however, were not reluctant to fish in troubled waters in Israel. Opposition to Solomon among his subjects readily found Egyptian and Aramean support; potential rebel leaders like the Edomite (or possibly Aramean) vassal scion were warded in Egypt until the right moment for revolt.

Solomon's pretensions to royal grandeur outran his means. He proved unable to control sufficient trade and territory to maintain the borders of his inherited kingdom and to support the conspicuous consumption of his court and temple. According to the biblical record, each day Solomon and his men and their families ate thirty sacks of flour, sixty sacks of meal, thirty oxen, a hundred sheep, assorted antelope and fowl, and unspecified quantities of wine and oil—all served up by Nathan's son Azariah, the royal commissary. But in his efforts to maintain his desired life-style, Solomon, who lacked David's experience of building power, failed to emulate his father's adroit juggling of tribal and court jurisdiction. By murdering Joab and banishing Abiathar, he succeeded in decimating what remained of tribal hierarchy in Israel and imposed state rule as uniformly as he could, thereby destroying the fragile consensus assumed by David.

The burden of maintaining Solomon's regime fell upon the villagers in his realm. In place of the tribal militia, which was already

becoming expendable in David's time, and David's mobile profes-
sional corps, Solomon chose to rely on a standing army of chario-
teers, mercenaries, and drafted infantry, all of which were both less
maneuverable and more costly than David's army. These forces were
led by Benaiah, David's commander, until old age. To provision this
army, the villagers paid heavy taxes for a force in which they had
no interest, unlike the tribal militia. They also paid by yielding to
conscription, which David had attempted and failed to introduce.
Solomon ordered great urban rebuilding projects, with military
palaces, administration buildings, oversized granaries, and a temple,
to be built with state-drafted corvée labor managed by the old hand
Adoram.

The centerpiece of Solomon's building program was the palace
and temple in Jerusalem, new houses for king and god. Solomon's
took thirteen years to build, Yahweh's seven. Palace and temple
were designed by a Phoenician architect and with much material
assistance from Hiram, king of Tyre. When the work was complete,
Solomon had to hand over twenty villages in Galilee, whose villagers
thus changed from Israelites to Sidonians in a wink, it being all the
same to them. In architecture, equipment, procedure, and ideology,
the temple's cult was indistinguishable from the cults of Baal and
other urban deities throughout the eastern Mediterranean. The
temple was dedicated to the dynastic succession, the inheritance of
rule within the house of David. The antithesis of David's modest
cult, it became the source of law and order for Solomon's kingdom
(though before Josiah in the seventh century B.C.E. its law applied
little beyond Jerusalem) and the repository of the Hebrew scriptures
begun by David, for one thousand years, less one short interval.

The temple was sanctuary, treasury, court, and archive. It became
the center of the nation's life under the rule of the house of David,
even though for all its grandeur it was the king's private chapel,
whose closest precincts were barred to all but the most wealthy and
influential. Its cult of priestly meat-eating along with generous pre-
bendal support freed its priesthood to pursue their duties as butch-
ers, cult petitioners, taboo specialists, vocal and instrumental artists,
scribes, lawyers, judges, counselors, prophets, and warriors. The
temple became a widely hated institution that possessed, however,
a deep reservoir of potential for purification, reform, and popular
loyalty, depending on the political position of the ruler of the day.

The function that integrated temple, priesthood, and scriptures
was not observance of the cult for its own sake, but the interpretation

and application of law (see, for example, 1 Kgs. 8:31-32). In the biblical world, cult and jurisdiction were always combined, in the smallest to the largest cults, since law was thought of as divinely revealed. At the temple, the priests, on behalf of the king, were the final arbiters of the state's standards, norms, regulations, customs, penalties, taboos, and sanctions in written form. These were what made up torah.

The jurisdiction of Solomon's temple, and its successors in Jerusalem, was of a particular type. Political geographers distinguish three levels of jurisdiction associated with three levels of political economy: imperial, state or provincial, and local. In geographical theory, this tripartite division is inherent in political organization. At one end of the scale is the local level of direct experience where the attention of most people is focused most of the time. At the other end is the imperial level, the most comprehensive and hence dominant form of organization and rule, which subsumes most activities beneath it but is of direct access to few.

The third, or state, level lies between the other two, where elites, or what one historian has called the "political nation," the ruling class as policymakers in the name of their subjects, carve out a sphere of influence, often in the service of local or imperial jurisdictions but politically distinct from them, bring under their control a set of local jurisdictions, and try to convince their subjects that they are secure. (The biblical terms for political nation like *am* and *goy* are often misleadingly translated "people" or "nation"; similarly, terms like "kingdom" sometimes might better be translated "ruling class" or the like.) In practice, jurisdiction was extremely changeable, but these distinctions had considerable validity and are helpful for understanding the development of the Bible.

The jurisdiction of the temple in Jerusalem for the whole period of its existence was of this third, in-between type. The temple and its scriptures stood at the center of divine authority in Israel and Judah, whose main ingredients were endowment, magistracy, and constabulary, or wealth, jurisdiction, and duress, and whose main effort as expressed in the scriptures was to dispel the political nation's fear of losing jurisdiction to the world's greater powers and to project the temple's jurisdiction over the subjects of Davidic rule. The Hebrew scriptures formed as part of these related functions of the state and, after the destruction of the temple, of the organizations that inherited its scriptures.

While David had made do with fixing up the best existing house for his palace and preserving a tent for worship, Solomon expropriated the city threshing floor for his mighty temple fortress, putting an end to food production in the city. Ancient Jerusalem was built on a spur protected on three sides by steep ravines. The threshing floor had been high on the exposed northern side, to catch the winnowing breezes. There the temple bulwark completed the city's defenses. Thus protected, Solomon enshrined the tribal battle ark in the temple's innermost sanctuary, never to be seen again by the ordinary, and presided over a generation in which, for the first time in Israel but not the last, the ruler's warfare against his own people went by the name of peace ("peace" being the meaning of Solomon's name).

Although David's scattered settlements of Levites, who traced their lineage to Moses, survived in the countryside, David's appointee Abiathar lost his position supervising the tribal cult. For the temple cult David's veteran priest Zadok, now also Solomon's national security adviser, whose family claimed Aaron as its forebear, established a state priesthood of cult specialists, a caste that, like the top echelons of the military, became hereditary. (Zadok's name continued powerful in Judah through subsequent centuries and appears in the New Testament in the name of the Sadducees.) The priesthood, again like the military, was supported with endowed lands. These were granted first from conquered territory, then as that shrank, from the Israelite highland, even though most of the military and priesthood were either Judahite or alien. Like the army, the temple priesthood had to be provisioned from the villages to maintain its central ritual, the priests' consumption of meat slaughtered in sacrifice, typical of many ancient Near Eastern state cults. Sheep and goats, the produce of pastoral Judah, were the sacrifice of choice in Solomon's cult.

In the process of formation, the scriptures of the temple and its priesthood had two complementary purposes, described by one anthropologist as conserving and reforming. The scriptures conserved social norms that because they were written, were hard to adapt to changing circumstances. They therefore supported the continuance of their guardians as a conservative social group. The scriptures also had a reforming function. One of the roles of the priesthood as an intellectual elite was to develop and preserve, though not as often put into practice, alternative views of the world. Usually such views were co-opted, or preempted, from the cries, complaints, demands, and dreams of the poor, just as in David's cult. The accumulation and diffusion of such alternative views were a function of scripture as writing. Writing guards skepticism from being completely swallowed up in the ruling culture, and can provide an opposition with a steady platform. This occurs often in the formation of the Hebrew scriptures.

In the villages under Solomon's rule, reality failed to match the picture of peace and prosperity portrayed in Davidic propaganda for the united kingdom of Israel and Judah. Villagers had to yield their land and labor to pay increasing burdens of taxation and debt. As debt slavery grew, land was absorbed into feudal fiefs used to support military forces and temple priesthood. Collective cultivation rights in the village were lost to absentee city landlords. Tribal patrons, once the villagers' defense against abuse of state power, were losing influence in competition with Solomon's urban landholders. But the tribe, though weakened in reality, lived on in the literature of the Davidid temple as a metaphor for the nation of Israel, and this tribal metaphor allowed the scripture imbued with it to survive and even support the reaction against the house of David and all their like.

Solomon's scriptorium kept busy producing the many administrative documents required to govern the realm and manage its international relations. It also contributed to the scripture produced by David's court. Having succeeded to David's throne by right of inheritance more or less legitimately, and supported by partners in his father's coup, Solomon did not require a new history to establish his right to rule. Wise sayings ascribed to Solomon and confirming the court in the propriety of its life-style were duly recorded, following the practice in the courts of the great kings of Egypt and Mesopotamia, inaugurating the collection of prudent sayings and observations, which much later in the Judahite monarchy developed into the book of Proverbs.

Additions to David's literary defenses were made concerning Solomon's birth and succession, thus completing 1 Samuel 15 through 1 Kings 2. David's apologia for his treatment of Saul and Abishalom were supplemented to show that catering to the tribal leaders and their discontents (now discovered to be a habit of David's) leads to turmoil, that Solomon was destined by his royal forebear's god for the throne, and that in his final words David sanctioned violence to install Solomon's authority over the tribes and called it "wisdom."

The chronicles of Solomon excerpted in 1 Kings 3–11 (1 Kgs. 11:41) were begun at this time.

Solomon's temple cult continued the use of David's liturgy, in greatly elaborated form. The original petitions were supplemented with declarations of royal power, including Psalm 2 at the beginning of the collection, a raucous salute to the pretensions of Davidic imperialism, Psalm 8, a paean to priestly prerogative, and Psalm 29, a hymn to Baal adapted for use in the cult of Yahweh. The concluding Psalm 72 (note its concluding colophon), attributed to Solomon, acclaimed the king's justice and the continued prosperity of his dominions, starting with his own table. This prayer united the collection and placed all under David's imprimatur. Other songs of the cult, like Psalms 96–99, which may have been added after Solomon's reign but express the style of his temple's cult, extolled Yahweh's kingship over alien ruling elites ("nations"). Psalm 132, celebrating the entrance of the ark into the Davidic cult, is likely to come from the time of David or Solomon.

Contrary to the impression given in the Bible, by ancient Near Eastern standards Solomon was a middling monarch, scarcely the richest or the harshest Israel ever knew. That distinction awaited rulers of later periods, in the wake of the full use of the iron rod. Yet Solomon represented a culture new to Israel. For the first time, political Israel possessed great cities, with temples, palaces, administrative chambers, oversized granaries, and standing military equipped to prevail in the lowlands, and suffered the wholesale dissolution of social bonds. Political Israel's tribal origin receded in the mists of time, its letter to be revived on occasion as a device of public policy, its spirit in every age in the denunciation of state oppression.

6

Revolution in Israel

Solomon's tenuously united kingdom fell apart under his successors along a fundamental divide between north and south. Judah in the south, the home of David's family, had been the base of David's rule and continued under the house of David. Judah was a hilly plateau circumscribed geographically, bounded by precipitous foothills in the west and desert to the east and south, smaller and less populous than Israel. Jerusalem remained its chief city through several changes of regime in Palestine and had connections beyond its hinterland so that it was not heavily dependent on regional support. As a rule, through the centuries the law of the court prevailed in the city, local custom in the country.

To the north Israel, by contrast, had more land, and more fertile land, and more people than Judah. It was therefore more agricultural than pastoral in its economy. As its boundaries were more open than Judah's and greater trade routes ran near it and through it, Israel was more subject to intervention by foreign forces. Politically it was basically a confederation of local powers based in towns and villages. The capital was usually located in or near Shechem in the north central highland, but was moved about. Customary law and local cult prevailed throughout: the law of city and country tended to be the same. Large landowning families dominated agricultural production and trade in cash crops. Factional fighting among them was hard to contain. Any king who would assert himself over this territory had to depend for support upon these magnates and upon local saints, the divinely backed power brokers among families, embodying the sacredness of social order, with no mean influence over cult, legal disputes over land and debt, military campaigns, food distribution and famine, disease, and disaster. (Though they worked locally, they often worked best far from their own home.)

Solomon's son Rehoboam succeeded to the throne undisputed in Judah but needed confirmation from the local magnates in Israel that was not forthcoming. His attempt to intensify corvée labor in Israel for the royal court ("My father disciplined you with whips, but I will discipline you with barbed lashes") was rejected by a coalition of villagers, magnates, saints, and some factions dissatisfied with Solomon's tyranny and backed by Egypt. In a bona fide village revolt, rarely depicted in the Bible, time-worn Adoram, still administering corvée for David's grandson, was stoned to death and Rehoboam was forced to withdraw. Escaping from forced labor for Jerusalem, Israel in effect seceded from Judah and the rest of Solomon's kingdom and gained a temporary respite from tyranny.

The throne of Israel was restored by one Jeroboam, who had been Solomon's corvée administrator in Ephraim but, becoming disaffected with his royal master, had taken refuge in Egypt along with other rebels against Solomon's tyranny and gathered a band of supporters around him in exile, just as David had built his strength among the Philistines. Perhaps opportunely he was thus absent from Israel during the anti-Adoram putsch, just as David claimed to have missed the killing of Saul and Abner, but returned, a creature of the king of Egypt as much as of the people of Israel, to be offered the throne by the victorious forces. His installation as king was confirmed by the saint of Shiloh, Ahijah.

Jeroboam's power base was wide but shallow, requiring careful orchestrating. Once in power, he had to avoid antagonizing the tribal magnates, while proceeding to exercise the royal authority of his models David and Solomon. He recruited some support among the rebels against Solomon's rule by conceding authority to tribal magnates, restoring the village militia, protecting villagers' legal rights against magnates, and respecting tribal custom. But he himself undertook a royal building program, requiring corvée labor (in whose administration he happened to be expert), in Shechem and Penuel, then moved the capital to Tirzah, his Jerusalem, just northeast of Shechem.

For the cult he refurbished shrines in Bethel and Dan, both pilgrimage shrines near the borders with Jerusalem and Damascus, his main opponents, possibly to cultivate support among the priestly clans, one an Aaronite line at Bethel and one tracing descent from Moses at Dan. As a counter to Solomon's eclectic state cult that tended to merge Yahweh with the god Baal worshiped in the coastal cities, he revived the cult of the tribal El behind Yahweh, also known by the honorific plural Elohim, a patron of agricultural production and fair judgment as good as Baal, but in no need of a temple and all it had stood for under Solomon. In contrast to the sheep sacrifice in the cult of pastoral Judah, anointing standing stones, or menhirs, with olive oil seems to have been the major feature of the cult, celebrating one of Israel's chief crops. The events in the festival calendar were returned to an earlier Israelite schedule to match harvesttime in the north.

Jeroboam's rise to power, as we have seen, paralleled David's in several ways. This meant that Jeroboam could read J, David's victory story of Israel's escape from corvée, perhaps available to him from a royal office in Shechem or Megiddo, as his own story, with Solomon and his successors in the role of pharaoh, and Jeroboam, belonging to the tribe of Joseph and with Egyptian court experience, taking the part of Joseph and Moses (David). Indeed, in J the house of David delivered a propaganda bonanza into the hands of Jeroboam. Here is the first, but by no means the only, use of the Bible story to defy the power that commissioned its writing.

So Jeroboam adopted the scripture of the royal house whose throne in Israel he had usurped; he also had it adapted to tell his own victory story. His revisions to the J document are known as E, standing for Elohim, the designation Jeroboam used for Yahweh in order to distance himself from Solomon's version of Yahweh.

The chief concern of E is to defend Israel's revolution in the person of Jeroboam and his judiciary, and to legitimate the succession to power by his son. By implication, it was to establish Jeroboam's right to revolt against the house of David. Jeroboam had been a fatherless child, and he probably had to leave one of his own sons as hostage in the court of pharaoh. At least one other son died young. Jeroboam was preoccupied with the safety of sons as heirs, and nearly every story in E takes this as its theme.

Moreover, many of the magnates who had just thrown off the yoke of one king were hardly eager to support another. They had an urgent question to put to Jeroboam of the tribe of Joseph: "Are you to be king over us?" In E, this is the question raised by the tribes when young Joseph told them he had dreamed that they were all out in the field binding sheaves and their sheaves bowed down to his. This question is answered in the rest of E's story of Joseph: the brothers devised evil against Joseph, but God devised that the same should turn out good in the end. The official history of Israel now showed that Jeroboam's rule was God's plan. In compensation, it also showed the cults of the magnates and their jurisdictions validated, and precedents from the customary law of the land defined in writing and thus ratified by the new Israelite ruler. Where J defined only cultic law, E's rulings began by defining the limits on debt slavery and went on to deal with the other categories typical of ancient Near Eastern law, thus raising royal jurisdiction to the level of that of the people's cults. Like all privileged, Jeroboam feared himself in other men, and hence projected this fear, in the guise of cultic and judicial respect, or the "fear of God," as public policy. This, too, is a major theme of E.

Although Jeroboam's kingdom was based in the north, in his scripture he made no effort to emphasize a specifically northern, or Israelite, tradition at the expense of the southern Judahite tradition fostered by David and Solomon. Indeed, E deals with personages associated with Israel and the north only as they relate to Jeroboam's own household and activities. This is the only reason for the emphasis on Joseph, patron of Shechem. Jacob, who stands for all Israel, figures in E only as a founder of shrines at Beersheba, Gilead, Mahanaim, Penuel, an oak south of Bethel, Rachel's tomb, and especially Bethel. With the exception of the first, these outline the probable eastern and southern bounds of the kingdom of Saul, when Israel was last independent of the house of David. Generally E avoids celebrating the tribal values promoted by J in support of David's royal rule to focus on the royal jurisdiction and cults of Jeroboam, the rebel against the royal house of David.

Just as he feared, Jeroboam failed to establish his own royal line on the throne of Israel. His son and successor was quickly overthrown, and after a series of coups and countercoups a military commander, Omri, seized the throne for himself and his family, where it remained, during the first half of the ninth century, for three generations, through four of the more notorious kings in the Bible. Omri receives scant attention in the Bible, but he was important, and it is no accident that he is the first biblical personage to be mentioned in an ancient document other than the Bible.

Omri and his son Ahab were no doubt bigger bullies than David and worse tyrants than Solomon. Their big mistake, however, was to fail to cultivate good public images by gaining the approval of a prestigious saint and by having scripture written or adapted to legitimate their rule.

The window in imperial domination of Palestine in which Israel was formed had long since closed. Resurgent Egypt, with whom Solomon had had to deal, invaded under Pharaoh Shoshenq (Shishak) five years after Solomon's death, but by the end of the tenth century had again faded from the scene, undone by lack of iron. Aramean (Syrian) and Phoenician cities wielded their supremacy. The dominant imperial power in the Age of Iron was Assyria, in whose shadow lesser states rose and fell. Under this pressure, tribal peoples either formed into states, much as early Israel had done, or fled from state organization into intensified nomadism.

The house of Omri took Solomonic measures to buttress the kingdom of Israel against rising Assyria. It formed alliances with its neighbors, principally Tyre and Judah (Omri's son Ahab married a princess of Tyre, Jezebel; his granddaughter Athaliah married into the royal family of Judah and reigned there for seven years herself), and expanded control over most of what had been Solomon's united kingdom, possibly even including Judah for a brief period. By heavy exaction of corvée labor, Omri fortified a new city, Samaria, as his new Jerusalem.

In Samaria, Omri fostered the practice of Phoenician urban maritime cults, particularly the worship of Baal, the patron of commercial agriculture under royal control and conspicuous consumption of trade commodities. The border shrines and the official cults of Yahweh-El, the patron of village polity and production, fell into neglect. With the decline of these cults went the decline of their jurisdictions, and of the customary rights agreed to, for the convenience of the monarch, at the founding of the kingdom.

The Omrids, for the moment the nucleus of western kings' resistance to Assyria, built up an imposing military force at the expense once again of the villages. Under Omri and Ahab, tribal sentiments could be pronounced dead. Omri's son Ahab commanded an army one and a half times as large as Solomon's, supported on a territorial and population base perhaps half as large. To maintain this army, the royal household expanded its control over more and more of

Israel's economy, impoverishing the villages and manipulating trade.

Life in the villages under the Omrids, starkly portrayed in the Bible, was an exacerbation of life under Solomon, whose suffering has to be read between the lines of the Davidic picture of a golden age. The royal household undertook to rationalize agriculture in order to maximize its intake, over the workers' dead bodies, to build up its export trade and provision its army. The lowlands were to be devoted to large-scale cultivation of wheat, the highlands to grapes and olives, and both to the raising of livestock required for labor in the fields, intensified manuring, and furnishing meat to court, temple, and army. The land was acquired for these agribusiness operations by accelerating foreclosure on debt, pushing farmers into debt slavery as soon as they failed to fulfill the obligations due for their use of the land, and consolidating small plots into large holdings or latifundia. The villagers' hardships were compounded by famines during the Omrid period, induced as much by royal policies in the distribution of resources as by shortage of rain.

Resistance to the Omrids in the villages is reflected in the popular tales of the deeds of local saints and prophets like Elijah and Elisha that circulated in the ninth century and appear in the Bible in 1 Kings 17 through 2 Kings 8. Such tales focused on the grievances of the Omrids' oppressed and exploited subjects, not all of them villagers, and with their miraculous outcomes empowered the hearers to hope for deliverance. For example, one of the Elijah stories depicts what must have been the typical plight of widows in Omrid Israel: war, famine, and royal incursion into the village economy wrecked their traditional support networks and the royal export trade drove up prices for staple goods, oil and meal, past their ability to pay. Many died. But in the tale, Elijah, an eccentric from Gilead tramping the Phoenician coast, helps one of these widows to discover in her own house sufficient oil and meal to keep herself and her son until the next good rains. Here Elijah demonstrates the saint's power to intercede for the poor—and rich—with the powers, earthly or heavenly, that bestow prosperity and to defy those that would withhold it. Later we shall see these tales organized into a cycle as part of the scripture commissioned by Jehu to legitimate his overthrow of the Omrids, and the prophets' role in relation to royal power will become clear.

7

Great Estates

The house of Omri, unpopular with its subjects who resented Tyre's domination in Israel's economy and politics, fell at last to external pressure. Shalmaneser III of Assyria forced Omri's grandson Joram to pay tribute. The Israelite king is pictured on the contemporary Assyrian Black Obelisk, dressed in Phoenician-style attire, with the caption "the tribute of Ja-a-u of the house of Omri: I received from him silver, gold, a golden bowl, a golden vase with pointed bottom, golden tumblers, golden buckets, tin, a royal staff, and a special wooden instrument [meaning uncertain]." Joram's capitulation left Damascus on the verge of being surrounded by encroaching Assyria. Damascus joined forces with Jehu, the chief Omrid army officer, to overthrow the house of Omri and tie Israel to Syria for the next forty years. According to Jehu's legitimation narrative, Yahweh sent the same saint, Elisha, to instigate coups d'état by both Jehu of Israel and Hazael of Damascus. For most of this period, the dominion of the king of Israel was overrun by Damascus and often scarcely extended into the next valley from Samaria.

Jehu's coup was thorough and bloody. In addition to murdering Joram of Israel, Jezebel, and Ahaziah, king of Judah, he eliminated over one hundred royal princes of Israel and Judah and slaughtered all the devotees of Baal whom he had gathered unsuspecting in the temple in Samaria. Jehu's men, with the support of at least one saint of Gilead, had him proclaimed king. (Although usually viewed as opposed to the state, saints often promoted notions of religious organization in harmony with the state's and when allied with a claimant to the throne could earn the respect of urban religious

45

authorities.) A massive reassignment of estates in Israel to Jehu's supporters ensued.

Once again the violent usurpation of the throne called for a document to justify the action to court supporters and foreign visitors. Jehu's scribe culled the royal libraries of Judah and Israel for models and combined them in a single document revised and supplemented to highlight the saint as kingmaker, a role adumbrated in the figures of Samuel, Nathan, and Ahijah in the stories of David, Solomon, and Jeroboam. Throughout the biblical period and after, holy men and women, saintly wordmakers who took the longer, less fearful, view, were active in Palestine, and political and social upheaval brought them to the fore. Their appearance named in the Bible at certain junctures is timed by their usefulness to the political purposes of the scribes whose writings became scripture.

The amalgamated history of Israel's previous kings came as prologue to the narrative of the legitimation of Jehu's coup, including, for example, the story of Elijah's slaughter of the 450 prophets of Baal. The whole is found now in 1 Kings 17 to 2 Kings 10. Jehu's scribe began by collecting popular tales of Elijah and Elisha whose scenes of havoc wrought by the Omrids formed the background to the appearance of the prophets' protégé Jehu as deliverer. Such stories, like that of the poor widow or that of Naboth's vineyard seized through judicial murder of its well-to-do owner by Ahab and Jezebel, appealed to subjects poor and rich who had suffered under the previous regime. The stories of Elisha also showed a solicitude for the armies of the king of Damascus, Jehu's angel. The scribe recast these tales, particularly those involving Elijah, who supposedly initiated the succession of Jehu, with several purposes in mind.

One was to demonstrate that Elijah indeed acted at the behest of the popular god Yahweh in protest against Baal of Tyre and Samaria, and that as sole agent of Yahweh in his day Elijah alone could appoint a legitimate king. Since Jehu's anointing took place behind closed doors—his followers saw only Jehu emerging with oil dripping from his head and a tale to tell—the chain of command had to be made clear from Yahweh to Elijah to Elisha to Elisha's nameless servant, who after the anointing promptly disappeared, to Jehu (and from Elisha to Hazael as well).

Another purpose was to suggest identification of Jehu's patron Elijah with the Moses of Israel's official history JE. Moses, ignored by the Omrids, was the symbol of tribal Israel and the formulator of the state founder Jeroboam's law and judicial organization. Jehu claimed a less direct, therefore more credible, connection with Moses than Jeroboam, by appealing to the common knowledge that saints might return from the dead. Again using symbols from the history of Moses, the scribe built on the tradition of genealogies of spiritual authority to show also how Elisha attained his right to lead the lodge of followers seen about him in the tales.

Even after Solomon's empire split up, Israel and Judah remained tied to each other by royal marriages, trade relations, and military alliances. Boundaries were fluidly defined by what fiefs an incumbent monarch was able to control and grant to his dependents. Thus for a time under Omri's granddaughter Athaliah, the house of Omri replaced the house of David in Judah, all Davidic contenders for the throne being held for dead. While Jehu held Samaria, Judah was to carry on the Omrid trade network and Baal cult.

After seven years, however, a priest of Yahweh, supported by the palace guard loyal to the house of David, produced a seven-year-old named Joash and declared him the surviving Davidid heir, a figurehead for a coalition of aggrieved parties. The temple having sponsored the return of the house of David, in time Joash renovated the temple to strengthen his own hand, a procedure regularly followed by ancient Near Eastern kings wanting to assert their authority. Under threat from Hazael of Damascus, however, Joash was forced to strip his palace and refurbished temple for tribute gold.

While Davidids maintained their hold on Jerusalem, the house of Jehu lasted five generations in Israel, a hundred years. For the last fifty of those years, after quelling a challenge from Amaziah, son of Joash of Judah, it held sovereignty over most of greater Palestine in a vacuum left by the withdrawal of Damascus from the scene after submitting to Assyria in 796. As Assyria was occupied chiefly on its own northern border, Joash of Israel and his son Jeroboam II, with Assyrian sanction, were able to regain lands Damascus had held for over a generation and extend their rule as far as Damascus itself. Meanwhile Amaziah, Uzziah, and Jotham locked in three generations of Davidic succession in Judah through coregencies like that of Omri and Ahab. Uzziah captured the Philistine plain, Ashdod, and the Red Sea port Elat and drafted villagers and tribespeople to rebuild fortresses in the southern desert territory of Judah. Jotham subjugated Ammon. In their latter days, the allied kingdoms of Jeroboam II of Israel and Uzziah of Judah rivaled Solomon's empire in extent.

This combined territory supported a thriving Palestinian export trade in wheat, wine, and oil, chiefly to the west through the Phoenician ports then at the height of their domination of Mediterranean trade. Jeroboam's orientation toward Phoenicia is reflected in the fact that the patron saint who predicted his successes was from the western part of his territory, Jonah of Gath-hepher, in Zebulon near the border with Tyre—while Jehu's prophet patrons had been from Gilead in the east near the border with his ally, Damascus.

The two kings collaborated in a commercialization of agriculture that surpassed even that of the Omrids. Uzziah rationalized production in the state-controlled lands of the southern foothills and coast, concentrating cattle and sheep in dry lands, wheat in foothills and plains, and grapes and olives in the hills. Jeroboam pursued a similar policy in the north. At this time oxcarts, rarely found in other periods, were used to carry increased produce from the villages to granaries and storehouses on the coast. More plentiful production of oil and wine was achieved through use of rock-cut presses for grapes and olives, then by the spread of the beam press, which permitted a second pressing of the olive pulp with a heavily weighted lever to produce lower quality oil for fuel and sale to the poor, after the first extraction by running water through gently crushed fruit.

The system of commercial agriculture imposed during the long reigns of Jeroboam and Uzziah had a dire effect on Palestinian villagers, especially in the highlands. Specialization of production destroyed the diversification of agriculture upon which villages in the higher lands depended for livelihood. Forced by heavy taxation on grain into cultivation of perennial cash crops, grapes and olives, farmers could no longer practice field rotation, fallowing, planting legumes to restore nutrients in the soil, or raising livestock. Meanwhile villagers were forced to encumber their land as collateral for loans at exhorbitant rates. As arable land was apparently more alienable than land in perennials, this was the first to fall into the hands of creditors. To feed themselves and their families, villagers then had to bring inferior marginal land into grain production, on which they got less food for more work and higher cost. Struggling with inexorable debt and taxes, small landholders lost what little land they had, and an increasing number became wage laborers and debt slaves.

While the state was procuring the maximum of wheat, wine, and oil through taxes and other exactions and its own production, villagers who could not raise enough food to feed themselves were forced to borrow silver against their future harvest to buy grain on the market when it was scarce and most expensive (winter). When the family had to repay at harvesttime (spring), grain was plentiful and the price they could earn on their own production low. Villagers starved. Meanwhile rich landlords impressed their labor to build second and third country homes and ate increasing quantities of meat. Livestock production fell almost entirely into the hands of royal and rich landowners, who got the benefit in plowing, transport, textiles, manure, and superior meat and even allowed stalled animals to consume grain, putting themselves at the top of a more complicated food chain.

The large landlords dominated local courts, where villagers might have sought relief from foreclosure. As the ever-fewer landholders became wealthier, the gap between rich and poor widened, and the social ties designed to relieve the burden of debt came apart. Absentee landowners congregated in the cities, especially Samaria and Jerusalem, and the traditional bond between patron and client deteriorated into anonymous exploitation.

The cults of Judah and Samaria at this time reflected the boom in agribusiness. Baal, the god of commerce, was widely revered. Under Baal's patronage as well as Yahweh's, nobles and warriors formed drinking societies, sodalities known as *marzeh*, to commune with departed strongmen, local heroes or saints in their own right, in orgies expending vats of wine and oil. Under the later Jehuids, who dominated the Samaria-Judah alliance, the shrines in Bethel and Dan nevertheless recovered importance. The demilitarization of Israel's southern border allowed Bethel to become the central shrine where Jeroboam II and Uzziah and their emulative clients could celebrate their prosperity. Local festival funds, supplied by individual villagers in turn, were requisitioned to finance the observances at the national shrine, at the rate of at least 10 percent of production regardless of economic standing. Villagers saw their resources siphoned off to advertise the pleasures of consumption to full and hungry alike and to demonstrate royal patronage of Yahweh's justice that patrons were to enforce for them.

As wheat, wine, and oil flowed out of villages and villagers starved in increasing numbers, Assyria was attracted to Palestine's efficient economy. Since the previous century, Assyrian influence had been growing in the region, although it was not yet a military threat. Near Eastern trade prospered under the twin umbrellas of Phoenicia and Assyria, whose economic benefit to each other persisted through the vicissitudes of peace and war. With the accession of Tiglath-pileser III in 745, the bubble of political stability in Palestine burst. Tiglath-pileser reorganized imperial administration, converting the Assyrian army into a standing army of conscripts, appointing governors over powerful landowners, and relocating rulers and elites throughout the colonies. On his borders some vassals submitted voluntarily to the exaction of gifts and labor, tributes, and taxes and became satellites. Others resisted and were brutally forced to yield.

Among the victims was the house of Jehu, rent by struggles over succession and vacillating in its attitude to Assyria. Some who gained the throne after Jeroboam II, like Menahem, paid tribute to Assyria; others, like Peqah, refused. In Judah, King Ahaz resisted joining an alliance of Samaria and Damascus against Assyria. In 732 Assyria overthrew Damascus. Ahaz paid tribute to Tiglath-pileser and visited Damascus to pay homage, from which trip he brought back a model of an altar for Jerusalem. Tiglath-pileser had Peqah replaced as king in Samaria and exacted a severe tribute of ten talents of gold and much silver. "Hosea [not the same as the prophet] over them as king I placed," he crowed; "he came before me to the city of Sharrabani [in Mesopotamia] and kissed my feet." When Tiglath-pileser was succeeded by Shalmaneser V in 727, Hosea, in concert with Egypt, took the chance to withhold the tribute. Shalmaneser besieged Samaria, and his successor, Sargon, took it in 722 and deported its rulers.

The fall of the house of Jehu and soon thereafter of Israel itself brought into prominence the words of prophets who unlike Jonah were not proclaiming Israelite success. They heralded the judgment of Yahweh, who was reportedly enraged at the state's oppression of the villagers and the collusion of the cult. Amos sentenced the ruling class of Samaria and their state to destruction. Micah did the same for Judah—as it then was. Micah described and Amos implied the impending redistribution to villagers of agglomerated lands held by wealthy landlords due for death or deportation and the prosperity that would result. In Micah's view the house of David was worth saving—as a defense against rapacious magnates—but in greatly reduced condition, with the Davidic city and temple razed and its land returned to its natural state. Hosea the prophet represented Yahweh as a father shamed by the realization that his wife, the rich city-dwellers of Israel, was the mother of children, their clients, fathered not by him but by the evil genius of agribusiness. Family bonds, however, would temper wrath, Hosea predicted: following punishment Yahweh would take back wife and children and make the land again produce food.

Isaiah, a counselor attached to the court in Jerusalem, envisioned like Micah and Hosea an end to latifundialization and imperial strategies and arms traffic. The temple, however, would remain the center of the world and its god the universal lawmaker and judge, to whom the reconciled and tamed heads of state everywhere were to repair for instruction in justice and peace. Given their differing views on the temple, it is not surprising that in the subsequent development of the temple scriptures Micah's divan, or collected sayings, remained "minor" while Isaiah became "major."

These four spokespersons from the court of Yahweh were clearly justified by events. Their predictions, read selectively by the surviving royal court in Judah, were used to gloat over the fall of Samaria and to flaunt the right of Jerusalem to inherit the title to Israel as in the days of the founders David and Solomon. Possible applications to Judah were downplayed. Micah, Hosea, and Isaiah outlived the fall of Samaria to add further to their pronouncements. Under the reform-minded house of David of the last decade of the seventh century, collections of their oracles became the basis of the writings that later played an essential role in enabling the house of David and its priests and scribes to come to terms with the fall of Jerusalem.

8

The Iron Empire

With the fall of Samaria in 722, the six-hundred-year history of Israel as a tribal and state polity ended. The vast majority of the people were still there, but most of a generation of the ruling class were not. The political nation was no more. They were resettled elsewhere in the Assyrian Empire, replaced in Palestine by rulers transported from other parts of the empire.

Under Assyrian rule village life went on as before, but most cities shrank to unwalled settlements, as Assyria, like later empires, instituted a policy of ruralization. Assyrian influence prevailed in architecture and other arts: traditional pillared houses gave way to Assyrian-style houses consisting of a courtyard with rooms on all sides. As in the late New Kingdom era in Palestine, pottery styles reflected colonial status: Assyrian-style, imported Greek, and local ware were all in use. Assyrian administration, like most imperial administrations, tolerated both the cult of Yahweh and those of the gods and goddesses imported with new rulers and allowed Bethel to continue as a border shrine.

Adherents of Yahweh cults in the north continued to think of themselves as subjects of their fallen capital city Samaria, for which the Assyrian province was named Samarina; later the people were known as Samaritans. The house of David, however, renewed their claim to be the native rulers of Israel, usurped, in their view, from the throne of Judah by Jeroboam I. This went on even when the house of David too became a vassal of Assyria.

The century following the fall of Samaria was the great age of the Assyrian Empire. A single dynasty ruled, founded by Sargon, who was followed by Sennacherib, Esarhaddon, and Ashurbanipal. In Judah the house of David enjoyed two long reigns, of Hezekiah (715–687) and his son Manasseh (696–642), thanks as much to Assyrian policy as to their own ability, health, and luck. During most of this period Judah's kings were Assyrian vassals, independent in name only.

In the reign of Sargon (722–705), the rulers of Assyria at last achieved their aim of controlling the eastern Mediterranean, west as far as Cyprus, into northwest Arabia, and toward Egypt. (Tiglath-pileser had already received tribute from west and south Arabia in 734.) Sargon organized trade with Egypt and stimulated commercial relations all over Palestine by the policy of resettling population. Coastal cities like Ashdod grew. Palestinian and North Arabian tribes were subdued to Assyria as the Israelite tribes had once been to Egypt: "I crushed the tribes, the Arabs who live far away in the desert, who know neither overseers nor officials and who had not brought their tribute to any king. I deported their survivors and settled them in Samarina." With control over the southern land routes, Sargon received homage and gifts from the monarchs of Arabia, whose states grew as extensions of Assyrian hegemony.

Hezekiah at first followed his father Ahaz's policy of keeping peace with Assyria, sitting out at least one major revolt by his neighbors. But after Sargon's death he joined a widespread revolt led by Merodach-baladan of Babylon against Sennacherib, newly ascended to the Assyrian throne in rebuilt Nineveh. All parts of Hezekiah's policy were then geared to buttressing his realm against attack. Along with administrative and military preparations, Hezekiah undertook a reform of the royal temple cult, a traditional means of asserting kingly authority, to dissociate his rule from Assyria's and bring Israel back into his pen. He refurbished Solomon's temple and appealed to worshipers in the north to participate in a national cult based in Jerusalem and sponsored by the ruling house of David. As a gesture of good faith toward Israel, he named his son and heir Manasseh in honor of the northern heartland and also revised the festival calendar to put Passover a month later as in Israel.

Newly issued laws reinforced Jerusalem's prerogative in matters of cult. "You shall not permit an unauthorized holy woman to live. . . . Whoever sacrifices to any god other than Yahweh [understand: as in Jerusalem] shall be destroyed" (Exod. 22:18, 20). Local cults sanctioning local jurisdictions not under Hezekiah's control were outlawed. A single law, as in Israel, was to prevail in both

capital and countryside, a significant departure from Davidid practice, which was to have momentous consequences in the production
of the Deuteronomistic History by Josiah in the next century. A
single saint, Ahaz's old counselor Isaiah, who commanded the king
to renounce armed defense and as an outcome of the impending
crisis looked for the reign of justice predicated in the temple's scriptures, was promoted as the patron of Hezekiah's reforms.

Assyria ruled its empire as Egypt had done, by dividing the population against itself and suborning local powers to keep central
power weak. While Assyria recruited Judahite strongmen to keep
Hezekiah under control, Hezekiah sought the support of the village
populace for the monarchy against their local lords. Thus he ruled
that "if you lend money to any poor, you shall not exact interest"
(Exod. 22:25). To appeal to the motley population settled in Palestine under the Assyrians, he revived the rule that "you shall not
wrong a stranger or oppress him" (Exod. 22:21).

Hezekiah's preparations for siege did much to keep Judah under
the house of David later when Assyrian power was at its height in
Palestine. He fortified and garrisoned selected cities in Judah as
depots for weapons and provisions. Hebron at the hub of the
Judahite highland plateau became the center of distribution for
produce contributed by all sectors of the population and sent in
high-quality storage jars, uniformly manufactured in one place, to
the fortified cities. Jerusalem, already well fortified, had its ramparts
reinforced. Just as the great Omrids and Jehuids of the north had
linked Israel's walled cities to their external water supplies through
monumental tunnels, Hezekiah ordered a tunnel cut through solid
rock beneath the city to a spring outside the wall. As the tunnel
was dug from both ends at once to hasten its completion, joining
the two was a first-class engineering feat. Its inauguration was
marked by what is today the longest extant Hebrew inscription from
the monarchic period, the Siloam tunnel inscription.

At first, as the rebellion spread, Hezekiah's efforts were successful
at home, and he enlarged his influence over his lowland neighbors
in Ekron and Gath. Eventually, however, in 701, his regional defenses fell to the Assyrian onslaught and the rescue force sent from
Egypt was ravaged. Sennacherib's stonecutters made the capture of
Lachish and its palace fortress, the most massive building from the
monarchic period yet uncovered in Palestine, the centerpiece of
their depiction of the conquest of Judah in reliefs carved on the
palace walls in Nineveh. After Lachish the rest of the land lay open.

Sennacherib's chronicle boasted that he attacked "forty-six of his strong cities, walled forts, and the countless small villages in their vicinity." The account concluded with the siege of Jerusalem. "Hezekiah I made prisoner in Jerusalem, his royal residence, like a bird in a cage."

Hezekiah bought off Sennacherib at a colossal price before the city was taken. Judah was engulfed by Assyria and remained in its grip for seventy years. Only Jerusalem and Hebron along with their shrunken hinterlands were left to the puppet rule of the dismantled house of David. Given his family's long-standing authority in Jerusalem, a compliant Hezekiah remained the Assyrians' best tool for control of the Judahite highland. Jerusalem in fact grew as agriculture benefited from the Assyrian peace.

Justified in his own view by the outcome, Hezekiah turned his ordeal into a propaganda victory. Jerusalem had been threatened with the fate of Samaria, but had been delivered. As Hezekiah's court presented it, this event confirmed the rights of the house of David and gave its temple establishment in Jerusalem the ultimate seal of legitimacy as rulers over David's kingdom of Israel and Judah. Hezekiah's scribe reappropriated David's history of the nation, J, in its northern supplemented form, JE, and made his own slight revisions in a prototype of the mixture of existing style and rhetoric in the temple scriptures, Israelite idiom, and contemporary clerical diction that historians call Deuteronomistic. We shall see it full-blown in the great history of the house of David's temple state produced by Josiah.

Supporting the court's interest in centralizing government and imposing a single law throughout the domain, the scribe made his largest addition to JE's law. Hezekiah's laws were as concerned for justice as those in E, but unlike E focused on prohibiting the practice of local jurisdictions and cults, for example the anointing of menhirs (standing stones). The final paragraphs of Hezekiah's additions exhort his followers to take heart in the struggle against the evil empire inspired by the model of the heroic Ephraimite sheikh Joshua (Exod. 17:7-16, 24:13), who was subsequently to become the protagonist of the Deuteronomist's mythical account of the conquest of Palestine.

Hezekiah's scribes also took over the house of Jehu's history of succession from Saul to Jehu, dripping with northern anointer's oil, and supplemented it from the extant court annals of Samaria and Jerusalem. The legal conditions on which Yahweh's patronage of the house of David were based were given greater prominence to explain why Yahweh abandoned Samaria and stood by Jerusalem in the same Assyrian assault; this device laid the groundwork for the adaptation of covenantal forms in Josiah's scriptures. The rhetoric of unity and centralization characteristic of the book of Deuteronomy and of the Deuteronomistic parts of other documents may have been initiated in Hezekiah's revision of Jehu's history of royal succession which became the basis of the Deuteronomistic History.

Saints, as we have seen, appear in the temple's scriptures at critical junctures to confirm the succession to power. In the literature generated around Hezekiah's maneuvering with Assyria, the words of saints announcing the ultimate realignment of power, the fall of a state, at home or abroad, gained special authority when states did fall, as many did to Assyria. Their pronouncements were recorded in divans—adaptable and revisable collections of speeches, oracles (often poetic), and narratives of the saintly wordmakers' deeds. This royal court form was the only way saints' sayings have been preserved.

Thus the fall of Samaria in 722 and later of Jerusalem itself in 587 each engendered a set of such divans, the "prophetic" documents of the Hebrew scriptures. Together these two sets address the fall of the states of Israel and Judah, under prophetic condemnation for their rulers' injustice, and the restoration of the Davidic temple in Jerusalem. These are the subjects of the Latter Prophets.

The compositions of the saints who had denounced Samaria—Amos, Hosea, Micah, and Isaiah—were eagerly received in Davidic court and military circles in Judah. In Hezekiah's time or soon after, Isaiah's divan was arranged around two contrasting foci, the responses of Ahaz (Isaiah 7) and of Hezekiah (Isaiah 36–38) to Isaiah's words regarding siege. Hezekiah's response was to credit Isaiah's vision of the rise of Jerusalem and the fall of Assyria. For Isaiah, as for the other recorded saints, at the end of the day no empire or even competing state would be left to interfere with the autonomous justice effected from the house of David's temple. This revelation, delivered by a court counselor to the king personally, was for consumption in cabinet, as long as Assyrian minions infested the realm. The form taken by the oracles of Amos, Hosea, and Micah in the court of Hezekiah has been partially obscured by their subsequent shaping in the court of Josiah and again in the court of Jehoiachin in Babylonian exile. Later, in the divan of Jeremiah, a story explained how Hezekiah defused Micah's unmitigated attack on the temple (Jeremiah 26).

Consistent with his dealings with Assyrian overlords, Hezekiah made prudence popular again. The court wisdom recorded under Solomon was supplemented by Hezekiah's sages and the book of Proverbs grew. Moreover, having narrowly averted the destruction of his kingdom by hostile enemies, Hezekiah conducted David's temple prayer service with fervor. It is possible that his scribes contributed some of the psalms "of David" now found in the second half of Psalms.

In the reign of Manasseh, Hezekiah's son, Assyria crowned its achievements with the conquest of Egypt, where it ruled from 674 to 655, thus extending a dominion for the first time from Mesopotamia to the Nile Valley. The strength of the Assyrian regime, based in huge military garrisons like the one recently excavated at Tel-Jemmeh on the southern coast of Palestine, ensured that a mere vassal king like Manasseh could enjoy a decent, orderly succession to his nominal throne and reign as co-regent for ten years and forty-five on his own. With no change in rule afoot, Manasseh played no direct role in the production of the scriptures. He was later exploited as the despicable foil to Josiah's Mr. Clean.

Real power over production and trade lay with local lords, among whom Assyria politicked, keeping the house of David weak by fomenting factional rivalry and preventing any major party of landholders from becoming attached to the throne. Manasseh, a loyal vassal to Assyria, looked for support against his magnates to local saints and sheikhs, and invited into his realm traders and their cults from the coast. The Assyrian guarantee of security also allowed the margin of settlement in Judah to be extended by floodwater-farming agriculture.

At the height of Assyria's power, Esarhaddon was challenged by Egypt, whose Twenty-fifth Dynasty aspired to reconquer the Ramesids' empire in Asia. Egypt began by subverting Tyre and Assyria's new fortress near Sidon on the coast. Having failed in one attempt, in 671 Esarhaddon led an invasion guided through the Sinai by a mercenary tribal escort (recall J) to capture the capital Memphis and proclaimed himself king of all Egypt. Although the pharaoh immediately took Memphis back, Ashurbanipal, Esarhaddon's heir, completed the conquest, marching all the way to Thebes, far up the Nile. The house of David contributed to all these Egyptian campaigns, and Manasseh named a son born in the year of victory at Thebes, in Hebrew *No-Amon*, Amon in honor of the event. Ashurbanipal appointed a new ruler for Egypt, the founder of the Twenty-sixth Dynasty, who by 651 had driven the Assyrians out of Egypt and reasserted claims to Ramesid Asia. Assyria's inability to hold Egypt was the beginning of the end for the Assyrian Empire, which drifted downward over the next twenty years.

In 626 a tribesman named Nabopolassar made himself ruler of Babylon and evicted the Assyrians. Within ten years Assyria was reduced to desperate defense against Babylon as with the help of western allies Nabopolassar pushed up the Euphrates. Ashur fell in 614, Nineveh in 612. Egypt came to Assyria's aid, hoping to stop a new star rising in the east. The remnant of the Assyrian army combined with an Egyptian force led by the pharaoh Necho was defeated in 605 at Carchemish by Nabopolassar's son Nebuchadrezzar. In this battle Babylon was supported by Judah, whose king Josiah Necho saw killed on his way to help the Assyrians. Nebuchadrezzar desisted from his pursuit of Egypt only when obliged to return to Babylon to succeed his deceased father.

With the Assyrian Empire suppressed, the Babylonian Empire took its place. For all but the ruling classes, they were the same thing. The fall of empire, however, did not go unnoticed in scripture. Nahum's and Zephaniah's announcements of Yahweh's judgment on Assyria proved true, so their divans joined Isaiah and the others in the temple catalog.

9

Josiah and the Deuteronomists

By the time Manasseh died in 642, magnates of Judah had long since carved out domains at the expense of the house of David, which was forced to share the taxes of Judah more widely than it liked. The magnates could blame the burden of taxation on the empire, while neglecting to mention the empire's role in backing them. If the house of David were to slip its Assyrian shackle, however, the magnates' rapacity would be exposed as the house of David rescued its popular esteem. Josiah (640–609) accomplished precisely this, and in the process had a hand in writing a quarter of the Hebrew Bible, the broad revision of the temple scriptures often called Deuteronomistic because it follows the ideas and style of the book of Deuteronomy.

At Manasseh's death, factions of magnates, some linked to Assyria, some to Egypt, competed for control of the enervated palace, while Assyria's rulers were content to watch the controlled undermining of the house of David go on. Eventually Josiah, the eight-year-old son of Manasseh's heir Amon, was elevated to the throne.

A canny youth, tutored by advisers who clotted into a faction around him, Josiah resolved to follow Hezekiah's example and reassert the royal prerogatives, and so set himself free from the grip of regent and magnate, and his nation free from Assyria, whose meteoric decline gave his cabal their chance. Egypt's help was never far away. In the year of Josiah's accession, the pharaoh began a siege of Ashdod that, according to the Greek historian Herodotus, lasted the whole of Josiah's reign. For a decade prior to Ashurbanipal's death in 627, Egypt occupied the southern coast of Palestine. Though hardly admitted in Josiah's scriptures (see, however, Deut. 23:7), Egypt and Josiah's faction made common cause against Assyria, at least until late in Josiah's reign.

Josiah made no effort to bolster Judah to the south or east. In his southern marches, he supplied Greek mercenaries working for Egypt, probably the first time since Solomon that the house of David depended on Aegean guards. To the northeast Josiah could not hold the fertile hills of Gilead, and to the east Ammon and Moab were under attack by tribes whom Josiah had no mind to challenge. Departing from royal tradition and historical precedent, he set his kingdom's border at the Jordan River. This boundary, in the Bible confined mostly to Deuteronomistic texts, so influenced the modern popular concept of the territory of "Israel" that it was used to define the British mandate and Hashemite territory in Palestine in the 1920s and thus the Zionist state of Israel in 1948, whose fixed borders (including the Occupied West Bank) are like those of no kingdom or province in the biblical period and, like the borders of all industrialized states, fail to represent the extreme variability of preindustrial dominions. For Josiah, the focus of attack was to the north, into the productive lands of ancient Davidic tenure.

As Assyrian power waned in the provinces of Samarina and Magiddu and in Gilead, Josiah began a series of military rampages that left resisters, whose tenure of land traced to Jeroboam or his successors or Assyria, dead, and joiners, if indigenous, with part of their lands confirmed—by their Davidic overlord. Thus much land fell to Josiah, who, wanting not just to demote the magnates of Judah but to make them join his movement, offered them liberated lands in Israel, to which the house of David had prior claim. Its claim was made clear in the greatest literary work of Josiah's court, the Deuteronomistic History, read aloud to preempted magnates invited to do battle for new land under Josiah's Joshua-like banner. Waverers in south and north found only weak support from Egypt, until late in his reign Josiah's success and Babylon's rise threw Egypt and Josiah into opposing camps.

Josiah devoted resources to conquest in a way Hezekiah could only dream about. As recounted in his own propaganda, Josiah's program began with the standard refurbishment of the dynastic temple. In 622, in the course of repair, a document containing a long-lost set of laws of Moses was reported discovered. A woman saint named Huldah was found to verify its authenticity. It was not divulged that the document, incorporating much archaic precedent, had been penned on Josiah's orders. Following the northern pattern of a single law for cult and countryside, Josiah promulgated this law based on E's model, the law of his refurbished cult, as the law for all Israel. The proclamation of a law of redress was likewise a standard act of new administration, as in the contemporary edicts of Draco and Solon in Athens. The heart of Josiah's law was its decree governing remission of debt: "At the end of every seven-year period, you shall write off all debt" (Deut. 15:1). This decree would have put a quick and certain end to poverty, toppling magnate creditors, if Josiah could and would have enforced it. With it and others like it, Josiah appealed over the heads—or under the heels—of the magnates of Judah to the villagers they oppressed. He offered villagers relief and restitution of their patrimonies, amounting to deliverance from their patrons, a pitch for popular support David himself could have admired.

The first and foremost of the discovered laws required that the cult of Yahweh, who was "one" (Deut. 6:4), be conducted at only one shrine (Deut. 12:1-14), the temple—where Yahweh would place his name, the basis of judicial oath. Following this radical decree, Josiah eliminated from the Davidic cult all foreign, especially Assyrian, elements and demolished local altars throughout Judah. The priests and saints of Judah's cults, clients and friends of Judah's magnates, were left in their localities, but deprived of their livelihood ate now at the pleasure, and from the supplies, of the king. Bethel, the northern shrine attributed to Jeroboam, the arch rebel against the house of David, likewise had to be destroyed. Josiah ordered the priests of Bethel slaughtered and their bones burned at the shrine to its permanent defilement and seized its treasures for the house of David. From there he ravaged the entire north, as far even as Gilead, wrecking every shrine and murdering every priest he could find. The jurisdictions of the north fell into utter disarray, to be reconstructed under Josiah's reform law. A new day had dawned—in blood.

In order to wrench the populace under his rule into the unprecedented channels required by the centralization of the cult in Jerusalem, Josiah decreed that the impending Passover and all pilgrimage feasts were to be held in Jerusalem, not at family and local shrines as always in the past. At the fall festival in Jerusalem that year, the new law, Josiah's law of Moses, was read out to the assembled nation, and a similar reading prescribed for every seventh year thereafter (in the interim it sufficed to know that the king would study it every day: Deut. 17:18-20). The law of centralization, and the carnage it justified, put the house of David once again at the hub of the amassing and allocation of wealth in Judah and Israel. Josiah's resolution and prowess had overwhelmed a host of opponents in the name of one God, one cult, one law, one ruling house, and one subject people.

On the seesaw of power, prior to Josiah the house of David had been held with its feet off the ground not only by the gentry but by the priests of the temple as well. Among these the Zadokite Aaronids established by Solomon ranked high. Hezekiah had enhanced their position by reducing the influence of priests outside Jerusalem or by losing the lands of such priests altogether. By Josiah's time, although the Aaronids like the Davidids had compromised themselves by colluding with Assyria, they had also enlarged their powers in relation to the ruling house. While needing to centralize, Josiah did not exclude the rural Levites from his cult, but ordered that they be supported in Jerusalem as subordinate priests, a halfway attempt to create a counter to the Aaronids. For the next two hundred years, the descendants of these Levites lobbied the dominant priests and Yahweh to grant them position in the cult, with privileges appropriate to the custodians of the law of Moses, while the Aaronids continued to abase them and to raise one barrier after another against their menace. In chapter 11 we will hear the voice of these Levites in full cry against their masters.

Josiah's closest priestly supporters, who represented a Levite lineage and tradition connected with Shiloh and Moses in contrast to the Zadokites connected with Bethel and Aaron, spearheaded the attempt to exclude entrenched priests from the king's inner circle. These included Josiah's chief deputy Hilkiah, made a chief priest, Shaphan, Josiah's scribe, and Ahikam his son, Jeremiah, probably the same Hilkiah's son, Shallum, Jeremiah's uncle, keeper of the royal wardrobe, and Shallum's wife Huldah, who had verified that Josiah's law was Moses'. For years, though their fortunes rose and fell, members of this circle influenced affairs in Jerusalem and saw to it that Jeremiah's pronouncements over a long career, reaching to the fall of Jerusalem, were recorded in what developed into the longest document in the Bible. But Josiah died in embarrassing ignominy, and the group never regained the dominance they had in the heady days of 622.

Led by Shaphan, Josiah's scribes undertook a full-scale history of the house of David—whose longevity now appeared matched by its strength—in the light of Josiah's triumph. Hezekiah's retouched JE, with its unpopular anti-Egyptian stance and its total neglect of Jerusalem and the temple combined with veneration of Jeroboam's Bethel, was set aside unchanged. Starting with the history of royal legitimation already on file, based on the original documents justifying David's usurpation of Israelite lands and including accounts of Solomon's glory and the numerous scandalous deeds of northern kings, Josiah's scribes produced the Deuteronomistic History in some five scrolls, Deuteronomy and the Former Prophets. Other works incorporated included some version of the deeds of chiefs and gang leaders contained in Judges 3–16.

Within the existing work, the main additions consisted of protagonists' prayers and speeches, didactic explanations by the narrator, and repeated formulaic censures of Jeroboam. As usual in such revisions, a new beginning and ending produced a shift in the work's emphasis. The history's main theme became the law behind Josiah's resurgence, how it was produced, used by Joshua to conquer the land, then lost, then refound by Josiah. Drawing on much earlier tradition and record, the additions determined the basic meaning of the work: even more than David, Josiah was the fulfillment of Yahweh's plan for rule by the temple and the house of David.

The history began with two new episodes adapting the figures of Moses and Joshua to the pattern of saints in the existing work. The history commenced on the last day of Moses' life, as he reviewed for the nation the history of their trek from Sinai (leave aside Egypt), which like E Josiah's historian called Horeb, after adopting the organization of jurisdiction going back to E and espoused by Hezekiah (compare Deut. 1:9-18 with Exod. 18:13-26). At Horeb Yahweh had appeared so fearfully that all Israel begged him to say no more, except to Moses, who now must declare the laws that will make it possible for the nation to capture the land, or they will be lost with his death. This crisis typified the Deuteronomistic concept of the crucial last chance at many junctures in history, reflecting the stark choices offered by Josiah's radical reform. Once disclosed, the laws were written down, and Moses died.

In the second episode, Joshua, the Ephraimite hero, studied the laws like a future king and conquered the land of Israel. Already introduced into the work by Hezekiah if not before, he was recast as Josiah himself in disguise, Josiah by another name. Like Josiah,

Joshua, leading the nation as one, attacked the heart of Benjamin, Galilee, and the Judahite foothills. Like Josiah, Joshua allotted conquered land to his followers.

Under Joshua, Israel kept Josiah's law and captured land. When Joshua died, according to Josiah's history, they neglected the laws and started to lose land. Even the law seemed to have disappeared. According to the incorporated history of Israelite tribal ruffians, well-meaning leaders, called judges and saviors, accomplished sporadic victories but, ignorant of Josiah's law, led the people to suffer one reversal after another at the hands of their enemies. The stories of the judges, in the book of Judges, represented the exploits of local and tribal strongmen of just the sort on whom Josiah strove to impose his law.

Of his laws, the first was primary: as one people to worship the one God at one place, as yet unknown. It took a king, and none other than David, the ancestor of Josiah, to reveal, by conquest, that the place was Jerusalem. Furthermore, keeping Josiah's laws required a king and an energetic house of David. Anything less was not, as the magnates might claim, loyalty to Yahweh, who in Josiah's laws prescribes a law-reading king, but mayhem, in which "each did what was right in their own eyes" (Deut. 12:8, Judg. 17:6, 21:25).

With the narrative of Samuel and Saul, the Deuteronomist reached his main source, which he left largely as it was. He composed a prayer for David on the occasion of Yahweh's promise to perpetuate his dynasty, one for Solomon at the dedication of the temple, and some other additions. Solomon's reign illustrated the glory of the house of David. His foreign alliances, relegated as a debacle to the end of his life, blemished his reign but did not alter its legal significance.

At Solomon's death Jeroboam founded the secessionist cult of Bethel, the most excoriable flouting of the law of centralization in the entire history. Josiah's historian cursorily cited the annals of the kings of Israel to prove that every one of them committed the same crime. Jehu's history of Omrid oppression showed the inevitable result. Even many Davidic kings of Judah violated the laws requiring purity of cult—no doubt because they were without the right laws. With Moses' law missing, its place was taken by the succession of saints representing Moses, as foreseen by Moses himself (Deut. 17:15-18).

The remedy to injustice—centralization in Jerusalem—had been declared but had to await fulfillment. At the instant Jeroboam had ascended to light the first sacrifice at Bethel, a nameless saint from Judah had stepped forward to proclaim, "O altar, altar, thus says Yahweh: A son shall be born to the house of David, named Josiah; he shall sacrifice upon you the priests who sacrifice on you" (1 Kgs. 13:1-2). It was only a matter of time, three hundred years. The fall of Samaria had verified Yahweh's judgment against Israel, but it had not put an end to the cult and jurisdiction of Bethel. The destruction of Bethel required an agent who could get rid of the Assyrians and their henchmen, and thus complete the ruin of those in Israel who persisted in violating the first law of Josiah.

The fall of Samaria, on which the Deuteronomist preached at length, and the deliverance of Jerusalem under Hezekiah brought the historian to the end of his base document. Hezekiah's pre-Josianic reform, from which Josiah had borrowed much, he passed over in almost total silence. The whole of Josiah's struggle to reconstitute the power of the house of David, the goal of the history, was compressed into a single year, tied to the discovery of the law in the temple—how it got there was not explained, the last reference to it probably being by David. In sum, the law of Moses emanated from the temple of the house of David in the reign of Josiah. Josiah lost no time carrying out its savage requirements. "Before Josiah," the historian concluded, "there was no king like him, who turned to Yahweh with all his heart, being, and strength, according to all the laws of Moses" (2 Kgs. 23:25, forming a frame with Deut. 6:5).

By transferring the judicial function of Bethel to Jerusalem and remarrying Moses and David, Josiah set the norm for the temple and its scriptures from then on. He did not, however, thereby create a constitutional monarchy. The law he promulgated was neither proposed nor imposed by the men who challenged his power. Quite the contrary, it set far more limits on his opponents than on Josiah. Their consolation was land in Israel. Josiah's revolution from above attracted support from the villages as well. The ameliorating norms of village custom made court law by Hezekiah were strengthened by Josiah, ingratiating him with his many subjects. This policy of making restitution to the poor, however, went against the tide of history as well as geography and could not endure as an administrative project or even as a standard for Jerusalemite law. As a prescript justifying jurisdiction in the eyes of the masses, later Jerusalemite rulers, royal as well as priestly, loved it.

In addition to producing this great history, Josiah's scribes worked on the prophetic literature to make some of the same points. They organized and revised the divan of Amos and possibly the divans of Micah and Isaiah. They also preserved two small collections of oracles closely associated with Josiah's policies. Zephaniah, a distant cousin of the crown, inveighed against not only Assyria but also the magnates and fellow princes who during the reigns of Manasseh and Amon genuflected to the empire and imitated Assyrian fashion. The day of war Yahweh planned against Judah, the original *dies irae*, was to be averted by removing the haughty magnates and leaving the "poor and humble"—Josiah's party among them—in peace.

Another poet concentrated his invective on one object alone: Nineveh. Saints were often known to pronounce against foreign powers as a source of the plight of the poor in Palestine, an accurate assessment. "Woe to the bloody city, all full of newspeak and stolen wealth, no end of plundered goods. All who hear the news of your collapse clap their hands over you in delight" (Nahum 3:1, 19). Josiah listened to this and clapped too. In 612 Nahum's oracles became canonical. The document was processed and put on the shelf in the temple library, next to other fulfilled prophecies relevant to Josiah's project.

Some of the divan of Jeremiah was first written during the reign of Josiah, and later added to, well into the next century. The accommodation with Babylon that characterized Josiah's administration left its mark on the book of Jeremiah, but in its final form it takes an anti-Babylonian, pro-Persian position, as do all the temple scriptures without exception, since that is when they received, with little addition or revision, their final form.

By the end of his reign, Josiah was sliding increasingly into the camp of Nabopolassar of Babylon. In control of the pass at Megiddo, he let Egypt slip through to Assyria's aid in 616 and 610. In 609, however, when Necho, having just succeeded to the Egyptian throne, marched for Carchemish, Josiah seized the opportunity to make a clean break with Egypt. He mustered his forces, took the field against Egypt, and died in Necho's presence at Megiddo—cause not stated. The aegis of the house of David was shattered forever.

10

Babylonian Rulers and the Court in Exile

The contest between Egypt and Mesopotamia over Palestine went on, with Mesopotamia still holding the upper hand. Although the rule of Babylon was brief, only sixty-seven years, no period was more important for the formation of the scriptures. The radical realignment of power involved in the fall of Jerusalem and the destruction of the Davidic temple generated a burst of rewriting history and recording prophecy that brought the Torah and Former Prophets and most of the Latter Prophets into final form.

At Josiah's death, however, the more urgent threat came from Egypt. Judah's resurgent magnates once again elevated a younger son, Jehoahaz, to the throne, on the understanding that he would keep his hands off them and Egyptian hands off him. Three months later, the pharaoh Necho, whose dominion at that moment equalled Tuthmose III's, ordered Jehoahaz shipped to Egypt. He charged Judah one hundred talents of silver and one talent of gold and installed Josiah's eldest son, Eliakim, whom he renamed Jehoiakim, to collect it from the country's magnates. Necho's days in Palestine were also numbered. Following the battle at Carchemish in 605, Nebuchadrezzar's campaigns over the next twenty years established the rule of Babylon over Egypt's tributaries in Palestine.

When in 600 Jehoiakim withheld the tribute he was now paying to Babylon, Nebuchadrezzar besieged Jerusalem. The city fell in

598. Jehoiakim died shortly before the fall and was succeeded by his son Jehoiachin, who surrendered the city three months into his rule. Nebuchadrezzar plundered the palace and temple but left them standing and placed Zedekiah, another son of Josiah, on the throne. Jehoiachin and three thousand nobles, priests, court functionaries, and artisans were taken to Babylon to continue the house of David's royal government in exile. The people, of course, remained in the villages in Judah nominally ruled by Zedekiah.

Zedekiah paid the tribute until Egypt returned to campaign in Palestine in 591. He hosted an anti-Babylon congress in Jerusalem attended by delegates from Edom, Moab, Tyre, Sidon, and Ammon, but only Ammon stayed with him for the rebellion, which prompted the second siege of Jerusalem. The city fell again in 587. This time Nebuchadrezzar killed all Zedekiah's sons and deported Zedekiah, as well as another thousand of the ruling class, to Babylon, where Zedekiah died. The Babylonians plundered what was left in the palace and temple and went on to destroy the buildings. This event, unrecognized at the time, was to mark the end of Davidic temple rule in Palestine, a watershed in the history of the Bible matched in importance only by the destruction of the second temple in 70 C.E.

The Babylonian, and later the Persian, crown appointed governors to rule Palestine. The first, Gedaliah, was not a Davidid, but apparently once a member of Josiah's and Jehoiakim's courts. A cousin of the Davidid family, Ishmael, connived with the king of Ammon and his Egyptian backers against Gedaliah, assassinated him, and ended up hiding from Babylon in Egypt, where some in the Palestinian community looked to him as the rightful Davidid ruler in exile. The saint Jeremiah was also taken to Egypt, though he anxiously backed Jehoiachin, the Davidid in Babylon, rather than Ishmael. Ishmael may have been among the 745 Judahites taken to Babylon in 582 when during a lull in his thirteen-year fruitless siege of Tyre, Nebuchadrezzar invaded Ammon and Moab.

Along with the forced resettlement of the upper classes, other populations shifted during the Babylonian era. With Palestinian politics in disarray, Arab tribes moved into Transjordan in considerable numbers, just as Edomites, on friendly terms with Babylon, moved into the Negeb and southern Judah. From now on this area remained in the hands of Edomites, who became the Idumeans of later times. Many villages south of Jerusalem, where rural life was tied to the capital, declined. In most areas the villages were untouched, carrying on their agricultural routines and prospering through the sixth century. The coastal areas continued densely populated.

The faction that had supported Josiah's regime pursued its activity into the reigns of Josiah's sons, although imperial control gave them less scope for influence. Speaking for this faction, Jeremiah agonized over the same royal presumption as other saints had in pressing for the rights outlined in Josiah's law. He urged and rationalized accommodation with Babylon. For him, as for other authorized saints, the fall of the temple represented not only the judgment of God but also the possibility of a new beginning. He was remembered as a gadfly to royalty, whose own career under the authority of others was seen to epitomize the tragedy of the political nation. In his view, when Jehoiakim and Zedekiah tried to take control of their own destinies and rebelled against Babylon, they brought on their own destruction. Jeremiah's predictions of disaster and his hope for the future were brought together and periodically revised over many decades to become the capstone of the Latter Prophets, to the advantage of Jehoiachin and sons and their court in exile in contest with Davidid pretenders.

At this time also the voice of Habakkuk was heard and recorded. He too complained about brutality and injustice in Judah and according to the written version of his oracles was shown in a vision that the Babylonians would sweep through and clean out the hoodlum strongmen perverting justice in his land. But, he asked, what gives the empire itself the right to play havoc with the Judahites, swallowing them down like so many sardines? The end of his vision showed bulimic Babylon passing away, wasted with overeating. In conclusion an archaic prayer expressed Habakkuk's confidence in national vindication to come. These pronouncements came into the hands of scribes who likewise decried the occupation, and when Babylon fell to Persia the fulfilled prophecies ended up in the priestly library where several short divans, including Hosea, Amos, Micah, Zephaniah, and Nahum, were being readied for inclusion in a single larger scroll.

Among the deportees in 598 was a temple priest named Ezekiel. As he saw his cult, land, and way of life polluted by alien invaders, his priestly sense of purity was devastated. Having lost his voice, that is, having gone unheard by the ruling class, he put on a series of mute tableaux to depict the disaster Judah's rulers had brought on their nation. His visions, like Habakkuk's, included the departure of Yahweh's glory from the temple in Jerusalem. When the temple fell, his voice was restored and his words became canonical. He also dreamed up a theoretical scheme for restoring the temple in the middle of the nation surrounded by its own land to support priests and by lands of the head of the Davidic nation, the rest of the land of Palestine being evenly divided among twelve tribes who would provide only token sums for the upkeep of the temple and court and keep the rest for themselves.

In Babylon the house of David was represented by Jehoiachin, the nominal king, who apparently enjoyed some income from royal estates in Judah. Although under house arrest, he and his five sons were not uncomfortable. About 560 his overlords allowed him to be restored to a position that a Judahite historian described as foremost among the subject kings resident in Babylon. The families of the deportees settled down, as Jeremiah had advised them after the catastrophe of 598, to build houses and establish households, plant lands, intermarry, and promote the welfare of Babylon. Their skills as artisans, scribes, and soldiers were well employed and well paid in their new homes in many Babylonian locales (thus in Nippur in the fifth century, Judeans are well attested in the financial records of the Murashu family). As they became assimilated to the dominant culture, they adopted Aramaic, the language of the northern tier of the Fertile Crescent that was replacing Assyrian and Babylonian as the language of the empire. People in the Davidid court assumed Babylonian manners and names: a son of Jehoiachin was called Shenazzar, from the Babylonian moon god Sin, later tactfully changed to Sheshbazzar, from the sun god Shamash, when the Persians ousted the moon god's devotee King Nabonidus; Jehoia-chin's grandson, who was to be sent to govern in Jerusalem, was named Zerubbabel, the seed of Babylon. While many Judahites in exile kept their identity with the cult of Yahweh, others patronized the cults of Babylon.

In the court in exile, priestly scribes continued work on the cult's accumulated documents. They made a slight but significant revision of the Deuteronomistic History. Among the mostly minor changes, an addition to the beginning (Deuteronomy 4) changed the emphasis of Yahweh's covenant from enforcing obedience to Josiah's law to offering the gracious opportunity to repent. A new ending updated the history of the house of David to the restoration of Jehoiachin in Babylon in 563, placing the blame for the debacle mainly on Manasseh and his cults (2 Kgs. 21:10-15) but partly also on Hezekiah (2 Kgs. 20:16-18). Scholars sometimes refer to Josiah's history as Dtr 1 (for First Deuteronomist) and Jehoiachin's revision as Dtr 2. This completed the Former Prophets as they now appear in the Bible.

Nabopolassar's dynasty ruled Babylon in the shadow of Persian power rising in the northeast. The last of the house, Nabonidus, resided at Taima in Arabia, leaving the capital and the state cult of Marduk in the hands of the crown prince, and in deference to his mother espoused worship of the moon god Sin. The priests of Marduk were annoyed by Nabonidus's religious policy and welcomed Cyrus of Persia to Babylon, as did an exilic scribe in the divan of Isaiah, as a deliverer. Cyrus took Babylon in 539, inaugurating the two hundred years of Persian rule in Mesopotamia that ended only with the conquests of the Greek Alexander the Great.

As the Persian armies advanced on Babylon, one brilliant scribe foresaw the change of administration—it was nothing more—in Babylon and declared Cyrus to be Yahweh's messiah. He urged his hearers to accept the announcement that Yahweh's plan for the overthrow of Babylon included returning them to Jerusalem. This scribe published his program by adding it to a slightly revised version of the divan of Isaiah, producing what appears now in Isaiah 2–55. He and his work in Isaiah 40–55 are known as Second Isaiah.

Resting on the successful prediction that Cyrus would take over Babylon, the burden of Second Isaiah was to persuade the second and third generation offspring of the deportees settled in Babylon to exile themselves from the capital of the world back to the provinces in Judah and Israel. This required a sustained effort of rhetoric unmatched in the Bible. The scribe chose to address the putative political nation, remnants of Jehoiachin's court, as the "servant of Yahweh," drawing on the imagery of the exodus from Egypt to evoke the notion of a new deliverance from Babylon, a deliverance few of his audience sought. The term implied that they should cry out as worshipers and suppliants to Yahweh to be saved, as the Babylonian priests cried to Marduk and were delivered. The term "servant" also suggested that like the "servants" who served as high officials in the Babylonian court, the people should be exalted to office in Yahweh's divine court, realized in a state that, chastened by the ordeal of exile, would broadcast and practice Yahweh's justice. This propaganda for restoring power in Jerusalem resonated with pre-exilic prophets' divans concerning the restoration of the temple.

Scripture writing in the Babylonian era was rounded off by the major literary product of the early Persian period (538–520), prior to the rebuilding of the temple. The Aaronid priestly families laid the conceptual groundwork for a revision of the royal history of Israel in their archives. Then, as with the support of the Persians they began to eclipse the house of David as rulers of Palestine, the priests carried out this revision, turning JE into their own legitimation document. The Deuteronomistic History was not suitable for revision, as it was in the hands of Levitical interests and spoke for Levitical prerogatives. The Aaronids took up the history of the nation prior to the reconquest of its land to elaborate on the cultic laws of Moses that went back to David's time, before Solomon's temple, by the addition of the rules for their own rites, often going back far into the monarchic period. The result was the priestly revision of JE called "P."

Changes were made throughout the JE history focusing on two issues: the complete reorganization of time and the calendar according to a novel concept developed under Babylonian influence, the seven-day unit of time (this is the origin of the week, one of few features of our secular culture that can be traced directly to the Bible), and the traditional priestly preoccupation with disposition of blood. Every cult requires an appropriate creation story. To represent these two issues, the Aaronids produced a new account of creation to buttress their restored cult, one devoted mainly to feeding Yahweh and themselves with meat at an elaborate tent shrine, akin to David's and ultimately El's tent. According to this account (Genesis 1), God made the world in six days and rested on the seventh. In the first three days God created light, the seas above and below, land and plants; in the second three days he created moving lights and moving water and land creatures. These move because they have blood. To keep moving they are appointed to eat plants.

At critical times in history subsequent to creation God made three eternal covenants of increasing exclusivity. By the first, made with the sons of Noah, that is, all humankind, people are allowed to eat animals as long as they do not eat blood (Genesis 9). The second, made with the sons of Abraham, that is, descendants of Israel, Edom, Ishmael, and other peoples to the south, prescribed the rite of circumcision that distinguished these people and limited the cult to men (Genesis 17). (Circumcision was in fact far more common than this.) The third, made only with the sons of Israel, ordained the keeping of the Sabbath, along with a set of other rules and taboos for the priestly cult dealing with the disposition of blood and the formulation of laws necessary for the purity of the land (Exodus 25—Leviticus 26; cult in Exodus 35—Leviticus 10; taboos in Leviticus 11–16; laws in Leviticus 17–25).

In order to counter the Levitical bias of the Deuteronomistic History, the Aaronid scribes made Aaron a hero equal to or greater than Moses and created their own version of what must be done to hold the land. Not yet restored to a rebuilt temple, the cult they envisioned was centered, like David's, in a tent, a tent of El revived with the tribal connotations but not the tribal politics of the archaic original. It was a cult of sacrifice, consisting of the slaughter, roasting and incineration, and consumption of meat. The taboos specified mainly what meats could be eaten, namely the flesh of animals that eat grass, not meat, and whose means of blood-based movement follow the pattern of the main herbivores of their class, that is, birds that have feathers and wings to fly, fish that swim with fins, animals like sheep that chew the cud and have cloven hoofs. Other rules governed cleansing rites to be observed after contact with menstrual blood, blood shed in sacrifice, and other bloodshed. The laws were filled out with detailed guidelines for legal and economic transactions. With the addition of a few further priestly touches, the Tetrateuch, the JEP document comprising the first four books of the Bible, and with the supplementation of Deuteronomy the Pentateuch (Torah), as we have them were completed. The authors of this revision were soon to be established under Persian hegemony as the rulers of Palestine in place of the house of David, with many of the Davidids' tenure privileges, as confirmed in JE, in their hands.

11

Persian Rulers and the New Temple

The Persian rulers inherited the Assyrian and Babylonian aspiration to extend an empire from central Asia to the Nile. They applied the familiar policy of asserting royal authority by buttressing royal cult to impose imperial control over conquered monarchies, just as they had done in Babylon itself in restoring the priesthood of Marduk. Cyrus's successor, Cambyses, who invaded Egypt in 525, was induced by collaborators to refurbish the dynasty's cult center in Saïs. Advised by the Egyptian priest Udjahorresnet, who received appointment as chief physician and chief scribe in the new regime, Cambyses expelled all aliens from the temple precinct, repurified the sanctuary, reinstated the "legitimate" priesthood, sacrifices, feasts, and festivals, while wiping out their rivals, and specified support to be donated by the Persian throne.

As the next ruler, Darius, struggled to confirm his succession, Udjahorresnet returned from service in the imperial court at Susa with a mission to undergird Persia's tenuous control by codifying traditional Egyptian law under temple auspices. The code, drawn up in Aramaic and Egyptian, exemplified the Persian solicitude for local law and custom as pillars of imperial stability that resulted in the Persian word for law, *data*, being borrowed into not only Akkadian and Aramaic but also Hebrew and Armenian. Udjahorresnet inscribed his own apologia in the refurbished temple, concluding "O great gods who are in Saïs, remember all the useful things accomplished by Udjahorresnet."

Much the same procedure was followed in Jerusalem. The Persians' first move in the 530s was to restore the house of David, in the persons of Sheshbazzar and Zerubbabel, but as governors, not kings. However, the Davidids were, unlike Udjahorresnet in Egypt, a disappointment to their Persian overlords, and during the imperial clampdown after 520 they disappeared, leaving Judean jurisdiction solely to the priesthood. The last notice of the house of David in government comes when Elnathan, the third Persian appointee as governor, attempted in vain to enhance his position by marrying a princess of the Davidic family.

When Cambyses died without an heir in 521, his successor Darius, from a different branch of the Achaemenid house, took two or three years to suppress the rebellions that broke out all around Persia's perimeter. During this lapse of imperial control, Haggai and Zechariah in Jerusalem announced that Zerubbabel and Joshua the high priest were to undertake jointly the rebuilding of the Davidic temple. By the time it was finished in 515, the house of David was out of the picture and the priesthood firmly in control, both the result of Darius's recovery. The temple was rebuilt in the name of the house of David, claiming Davidic legitimacy and preserving the Davidic scriptures, even though immediately the high priesthood superseded the monarchy as the main governing office in the Persian province of Judea (making P the concluding legitimating revision of the Torah). From now until the fall of this temple in 70 C.E. the high—high in contrast to chief, indicating additional authority—priest would be the judicial head of all Judeans.

Darius created the most powerful and integrated empire yet seen in the Near East, stretching from the Indus to the Danube, from Libya to Russia. According to Herodotus, it was divided into twenty satrapies, themselves subdivided into provinces and garrisoned by troops recruited from all over the empire. With road networks, coinage and banking systems, enlarged seaports and military fortresses, an efficient tax and toll collecting system, and a universal imperial Aramaic, the Persian regime created a common arena in which production thrived and many prospered. Like previous imperial rulers, the Persians enforced dependence by deporting and relocating portions of the population, both rulers and military garrisons (at a Judean garrison in the satrapy of Egypt, which may have predated Persian rule, numerous Aramaic documents have been discovered), with the added feature that they created quasi-ethnic enclaves for purposes of administration and tax collection.

Settlement declined in the north of Palestine, but increased in Judah in the early Persian period as population moved into rural areas, some never settled before.

The Persians collected taxes on as much trade as they could and promoted the ideal, picked up by their clients in Jerusalem, of interdependence, that is, loyalty to Persia, as the only source of wealth. Their dominance in the eastern Mediterranean, however, soon met a challenge from the Greeks, whose stimulus of mercantile activity in the empire first benefited but later threatened Persia's tributary income. The Greeks, recovering from the collapse of Mycenean power, had by now spread widely in the eastern Mediterranean and established an enduring power base in the Levant. Many Persian subjects, notably the tribes of Arabs now moving into settled areas along the arc of the Syrian desert, from Sinai through the Negeb, Palestine, Transjordan, Syria, and the Middle Euphrates, managed to bypass the Persians and deal directly with the Aegean powers. An Arab chiefdom that extended into eastern Egypt through the "land of Goshen," where David's scribe had placed the Israelite tribes in J, had access to ports outside Persian Phoenicia. The exemption of Arabs from Persian commercial taxes and conscription suggests elasticity in imperial control. The Arabs paid only an annual "gift" of thirty tons of frankincense and served in the military for hire.

The Persian wars against Greece, highlighted by the Greek repulse of Darius at Marathon in 490 and defeat of Xerxes' invasion by the Athenian fleet at Salamis in 480 and culminating in the founding of the Athenian Empire, involved Palestine and Egypt as well. Archaeology shows that Palestine, particularly Judea, lay on the watershed between Persian and Greek spheres of influence during their half century of struggle for hegemony in the eastern Mediterranean. To the east, in the southern hills of Palestine and Transjordan, local Palestinian and Near Eastern culture prevailed. In the west, in Galilee and on the coast, wide trading contacts came under Greek, Cypriot, and Athenian influence. In Jerusalem the Aaronid priests put their family interests as large landholders ahead of temple interests and tied into the Athens-Arab trade network for personal gain.

Persia's response to the Greek threat was to put its local governors under tougher political supervision. Just after the Greeks helped Egypt recover their capital from the Persians in 459 and with it the

Palestinian coast, the priest Ezra was appointed Persian high commissioner for Judean affairs and sent to Judea with an armed guard and a mass of silver and gold contributed by the throne and by wealthy Judeans in Babylon to refurbish the temple, that is, reassert Persian-style law and order in Jerusalem. Ezra's mandate included reorganizing the entire judicial system of Judea, reconfirming the temple-based Aaronid law of Moses as distinct, according to Persian policy, from the Persian civil law, and restoring the service of the temple, exempting all its priests and other officiants from Persian taxes. All this is explained in the book of Ezra, which contains the first signs of the use of Aramaic in place of Hebrew for writing scripture. (In Jerusalem the Aramaic script replaced the Hebrew script during the Persian period; the script known the world over as "Hebrew" is in fact descended from this Persian Aramaic script.)

The Treaty of Kallias between Persia, Egypt, and Athens in 448 allowed Persia to return to ordering unruly Judea. The court sent an expatriate Judean named Nehemiah, a high official close to the Persian crown, as governor (445–432), with a picked military escort to reinforce Ezra's flagging mission, reestablish Jerusalem as a fortress, and impose Persian order from the temple out on the Judean people. Nehemiah inflicted stiff corvée duty on the populace to refortify Jerusalem in defiance of local warlords. This work force of villagers was kept in Jerusalem day and night and armed against proclaimed foreign subversion. To defuse their resentment, Nehemiah followed Josiah's policy of hearing their complaints against their patrons, the wealthy priests and magnates, against whom the temple was not protecting them. He republished the Levites' temple law, with its provisions for remission of debt, reversion of land to former owners, and outlawing of exorbitant interest rates, and required the magnates to ratify it. Nehemiah also reinstituted a pilgrimage feast, the feast of booths, and the 10 percent tax on produce to support the temple cult. In the interests of extending administrative control, he conducted a census.

Persia's governors in Judea were expected to see that the commercial bonds draining wealth away from Persia toward Greece were cut and that the Judean economy was reintegrated with the empire's tributary system. Ezra and Nehemiah therefore ruled against marriage alliances between Judahites and families of the coast and Athens-influenced interior. Nehemiah used the census to resettle one tenth of every village into Jerusalem, creating a new urban fortress population under his control and keeping the villages hostage to him. Local trade was strictly regulated: the rebuilt city walls were opened only at midday to admit non-Judean traders and the Sabbath ban on trade was enforced on everyone, Judean and non-Judean alike. Commerce, especially foreign trade, was denigrated as contrary to tributary interests; economic activity was relegated to despised and powerless social outcasts, thereby undermining merchants' power.

Additions made to Isaiah at this time reflect this policy. In keeping with the original divan, the poet envisioned the temple as the hub of a global stream of tribute, the "wealth of nations," flowing on, by implication, to the Persian capital. Adam Smith, champion of capitalist economic theory, later applied this phrase to the very commercial wealth that the Judean client of imperial Persia decried. The Isaiah scribe also foresaw scattered Judeans streaming back to Jerusalem, not so much the exiles returning from deportation as the trading representatives recalled from travel in the Athenian Empire on business that was sapping temple and imperial wealth.

Representatives of these trading networks reaching beyond Persian Judea in all directions, such as Sanballat of Beth-horon near the coast, the governor of Samaria and Ashdod, Tobiah, strongman of Ammon, and Geshem the Arab, tried to counter the new regime by discrediting Nehemiah with his Persian masters. The book that bears his name is Nehemiah's defense before Yahweh and the Persian court against the charge of subversion and an epitome of the pro-Persian stance of the developing temple scriptures. At the conclusion of his public record placed in the Jerusalem temple, Nehemiah cried, like Udjahorresnet in Saïs, "Remember me, O my God, for good."

When the Persians gave up on the house of David in Palestine, the temple and its offices were left as the sole source of Judean jurisdiction. The priesthood, dominated by a surviving sector of Zadokite Aaronids, struck their own deal with the Persians. With no royal court to distribute land to its vassals, priests took over royal land attached to temple offices and became major landholders and commercial operators. The supreme priestly family, the Aaronids, became surrogate royalty; to most of his subjects, the high priest chosen from that family was king in all but name.

The law at this stage was in two parts: the Aaronid law in the four scrolls of the main cult history JEP, and the law in the Deuteronomistic History, held at Josiah's behest by the Levites, but now, lacking protection from the house of David, under Aaronid control.

To avoid the implication of two laws and prevent Levite scribes from taking liberties with the main history, the Aaronids had the scribes join Deuteronomy to the Tetrateuch of JEP, thus forming the five-scroll Pentateuch, the canonical Torah. Its conclusion in Deuteronomy 34 made Moses the greatest of the saints, the first of several maneuvers to neutralize the saints as foci of discontent. Although this revision was not immediately accepted, by the time of Ezra and Nehemiah, the "laws of the temple" were understood as a composite. Thus when the Levites succeeded in recording Aaronid injustice in Isaiah (using explicit language but veiled referents), they claimed to be the true keepers of the law by virtue of their adherence to the law of the Sabbath, a principle based on the Aaronid section, P, not their own Deuteronomistic work.

Despite tension with Aaronids, the Levites continued to carry out their ancillary functions in the cult as cleaners, porters, cooks, and servants of priests. As liturgists and musicians they performed the elaborate service of choral song that David's prayer service had become. They assisted the priests in managing the temple treasury, the repository of Judea's public wealth, of private funds, tax-exempt donations to the temple, and of notarized contracts regarding inheritance, land tenure, and debt. They kept custody of the temple scriptorium and library. As they had been Josiah's rural priests, they continued their profession of interpreting the law of the village, for the increasing number of villages that appeared during this period. Their prestige thus was based on their promotion of what gave Judah the little autonomy it had, the extension and application of ancestral laws and customs as widely as possible at the expense of imperial jurisdiction. Later the legal and scribal functions, as opposed to the menial ones, would be taken over by a class of scribes, and later still also by a group of free-lance teachers called pharisees.

Under Levite custody, the temple scriptorium set about producing the history of the temple and its cult that the new circumstances of rule without the Davidids required. The Aaronid cult history JEP, the Torah, still omitted to mention the temple; the Deuteronomistic History, now truncated of its first scroll, was preoccupied with the dead issue of Jerusalem's right against the usurpers of the north and included some scurrilous tales about the temple's founders David and Solomon. Apparently drawing on archival material previous scribes had missed or ignored (the Greek translation was to be called the "Things Left Out"), the interpretive revision of the

Deuteronomistic History that appears following Ezra and Nehemiah in Chronicles remedied these defects.

Chronicles linked the Torah to the temple by summarizing the Torah history in a series of extensive genealogies. The tent shrine of JEP was firmly equated with the temple: "the temple of Yahweh, the temple that was then a tent" (1 Chr. 9:23, assuming the phrase is not a gloss or conflation of two variant texts). Expurgated of unseemly incidents (for example, the circumstances of Solomon's birth), David's life story made clear that he had instructed Solomon in detail about the offices and services of the temple, in particular the role of the Levites. The secession of the northern kingdom was recast as a continuing rebellion against the enduring southern state, by overlooking all northern rulers except those loyal to the south. Hezekiah's refurbishment of the temple, always an absolute good, earned good press for his reform. And the history made extensive reference to the Levites, who had received but passing mention in Deuteronomy. Levite devotion and enthusiasm were credited with the nation's greatest triumphs; their songs of praise and deliverance were the new prophecy. Bolstered by fulfillment in the Persian restoration, they restressed the theme of exilic Deuteronomy: "If my people humble themselves, and pray and seek my favor [by maintaining the temple service], and turn from their wicked ways, then I will hear from heaven, and will forgive their sin and heal their land" (2 Chr. 7:14). The history concluded with the edict of Cyrus relaunching the Levites' temple, which confirmed that the Persian emperor, inspired by Yahweh, was the builder of the second Davidic temple.

As part of their restoration of the temple prayer service of the monarchic period, the Levites produced the second major stage of the book of Psalms. Setting aside psalms lauding Yahweh's lordship over the nations as incompatible with Persian suzerainty (Psalms 93, 96–99, though not 47), they added many more to produce what is now Psalms 2–89. They divided the Davidic psalms into two sets, 2–41 and 51–72, and assigned the Levites' psalms to three musicians, "sons of Levi," arranged to frame the second Davidic set. The eldest, Asaph, was placed at the center, Psalms 50 and 73–83, the younger, Qorah, around his at Psalms 42–49 and 84–88 (less 86), and Ethan, the youngest, at the end, Psalm 89. (These were later identified with the Ezrahite "teachers of wisdom" of 1 Kings 4 when the Psalms had lost their liturgical function and become works for study and meditation.) The Levitical additions began by stating the prophetic motif that God ranks justice above sacrifice and prefers thanksgiving for deliverance to the flesh of bulls, Psalm 50. They answered this challenge to the temple cult of sacrifice in a supplemented Psalm 51, admitting the irrelevance of burnt offerings to true sacrifice but anticipating that within the rebuilt walls of Jerusalem (to be accomplished by the Levites' protector Nehemiah) sacrifice would again be offered.

Among Levitical psalms, expressions of grievance at the injustice of the destruction of the temple and appeal for its restoration preponderated (Psalms 44, 74, 79, 80, 83, 85, 89). This type, popular in other ancient Near Eastern cultures as well, would seem to make sense as prayers of the royal court in exile in the previous century. Some may have originated there. With the temple and service restored thanks to the Persians, they became examples of prayers answered, a source of support for the temple and the Levites. Levites also favored hymns celebrating Zion as Yahweh's holy, impregnable habitation (Psalms 46, 48, 76, 84, and 87). These two types make up more than half the Levitical input.

The Levitical psalm collection also expressed veneration of the house of David, their crumbling bulwark against the Aaronid landed aristocracy. The first psalm in the collection, placed there by Solomon, referred to the birth of a Davidic king: "I Yahweh have set my king on Zion, my holy hill. . . . You are my son, today I have begotten you" (Ps. 2:6-7). Despite its political improbability, this promising motif was restated in Psalm 89, the concluding Levitical psalm: "I will make David the firstborn, the highest of the kings of the earth" (v. 27). Levite loyalty to their true protectors, the Persian imperium, prevented these expressions, like the Levites' extension of jurisdiction, from being considered subversive.

The smaller divans in the Levites' scriptorium invited gathering into a larger single scroll, the complex of twelve prophets. Scribes brought together Hosea, Amos, Micah, Nahum, Habbakuk, and Zephaniah and arranged them in chronological order, except that Hosea came before the oldest, Amos, because according to Hosea 1:2, "Yahweh first spoke through Hosea." In this collection oracles against foreign powers served the same function of legitimating Jerusalem as in the divans of Isaiah, Jeremiah, and Ezekiel.

Amos inspired the recording or composition of three documents related to it: Joel, Obadiah, and Jonah. Joel was an elaboration of the parade of judgments against foreign powers in Amos 1 and 2. These were understood to fall in the "valley of decision" where

"Yahweh roared from Zion and uttered his voice from Jerusalem" (Joel 3:16 = Amos 1:2). Joel made the salvation of the nation hinge on the intercession of priests. Whereas in former times, according to the temple histories, local saints used to make such intercessions and to chasten ruling classes, now, just as Moses wished, all can be saints, prophesying in chorus like the Levitical choir the downfall of Judah's enemies. "I will pour out my spirit upon all, your sons and daughters shall pronounce like saints, your old men shall dream dreams and your young men shall see visions. Even the slaves will join in unison." There would be little chance to challenge the existing order under these circumstances, or to say that the will of God might differ from the will of the priesthood. Nor would these loyal Persian subjects have occasion to sentence their foreign rulers to destruction.

Deprived of their function in the legitimation of rule, local holy men and women no longer found a place in temple scriptures. Temple legitimation was determined not at home in Palestine but in the imperial capital, Ecbatana, Susa, Persepolis, later Alexandria, Antioch, or Rome. Prophets did not all die out in 515; they lost access to the scriptures guarded by priests who found their pronouncements irrelevant. Even the Deuteronomistic History had had little to say about legitimating saints in the south once Samuel and Nathan had proclaimed David king and his dynasty permanent. In Chronicles, local saints of the south were introduced speaking to the kings of Judah, embodying the basic form of divine speech to the house of David as well as to the kings of Israel. Levites were also said to prophesy. Thus, in the absence of a king, Levites would communicate the divine will to the nation.

The foreign powers doomed by the oracles associated with Amos were Persian Jerusalem's trade rivals. Joel singled out the enemies emphasized in the Persian-period revision of Amos, Tyre and Edom (Idumea), which controlled coastal trade to the north and south, and added to them the Philistine coast. The end of Amos, also from the Persian period, named Edom alone for judgment (Amos 9:12). The oracle of Obadiah against Edom alone therefore followed immediately after Amos.

The book of Jonah, Jeroboam II's saint, was a fanciful story based on the completed divan of Amos. It accounted for Yahweh's inconsistent reversal in Amos, from condemning Judah to delivering it, by showing that since to reject God's mercy is more absurd than to accept it, the only appropriate alternative is to accept. Jonah's foolish repudiation of God's mercy made Amos's oracle of the restoration of Judah, and God's inconsistency, valid.

The set of documents, Hosea-Joel-Amos-Obadiah-Jonah-Micah-Nahum-Habakkuk-Zephaniah, drawn together under the same auspices as Chronicles, Ezra, and Nehemiah, served as the preface to the books of Haggai and Zechariah 1–8, which dealt with the restoration of the temple. The entire prophetic complex declared that the legitimate outcome of the history of God's judgment leading to the fall of the temple, as well as the ultimate will of God according to the prophets' revealed word, was the rebuilding of the temple. And the scribes knew whom to thank for this blessing. Though replete with oracles against every sort of ruler, temple scriptures expressed not one word of condemnation of Persia or any other ruling empire after the Babylonians. According to Darius's order, prayers were to be offered in the temple daily for himself and his sons. "If anyone alters this edict," he added, "a beam shall be pulled out of his house and he shall be impaled on it, and his house will be made into a manure pit" (Ezra 6:11).

The Levites undertook another revision of the already pro-temple, pro-Persian divan of Isaiah. This revision, referred to above, comprises Isaiah 56–66, so-called Third Isaiah. It voices the complaints of lesser priestly families, who despite their loyalty to Persia still suffered hardship as they had since Josiah's day, while the ruling Aaronids prospered. Maintaining their interest in keeping the whole of the law of Moses, including the remission of debt and return of land to rightful owners, they accused the Aaronids of dealing with the Arab and Edomite traders included in Abraham's covenant but excluded from God's covenant with Israel. Protected by Nehemiah's rule, they were able to turn the Aaronids' law against them, proclaiming it better to be a Sabbath-keeping eunuch than a circumcised dealer with Persia's enemies (Isa. 56:1-8): Abraham may be the archetypical father, as his name says, but just rule by nonfathers, Persian Judean eunuchs like Nehemiah who profess Yahweh as their father, would benefit the temple far more than the fraud of the priests in power. (This is one of the few places in the Hebrew scriptures where God is referred to as a father.) Family connections were mistrusted by the Persians, who ensured that their officials would have no posterity. Disrupted by Nehemiah, such connections counted for little in a society that commended with "power [phallus] and honor" (Isa. 56:5; Revised Standard Version: "a monument and a name") the eunuch and foreigner who kept the Sabbath, implying

Persian control of wealth, and through the Sabbath the whole temple law. Despite the ban on mixed marriages, the envisioned covenant community was not to be ethnically pure, but based on keeping the temple law defined by Persian administration. A similar set of oracles in Zechariah and Malachi concluded the twelve.

Also in the Persian period, Esther was written and introduced among the scriptures to illustrate the benefits of loyalty to Persian administration, even in the face of persecution. The Babylonian names Esther (Ishtar) and Mordecai (Marduk) show assimilation to life in the imperial capital. Ruth showed that the loss of family relations need not be the end of the world, since the house of displaced persons can join in the prosperity of a new locale. Job is a long poem of a standard genre ostensibly dealing with the suffering of the innocent, recast to depict a wealthy Idumean or Hijazi sheikh who enriched himself in trade outside the Persian Empire. He thinks he is righteous, but God puts in an awesome appearance to inform Job he has no right to decide the issue. In answer to Proverbs, now also reaching final form, which suggested that definable prudent behavior may ensure prosperity, Job acknowledged that God had the right to be capricious. By implication, the just complaints of the poor risked similar evasion.

During the late fifth and fourth centuries, Persian rule in Palestine weakened. Egypt broke free and fomented unrest there and in Phoenicia and Cyprus. Sanballatids still ruled Samaria and Tobiads in Ammon. On two occasions the high priestly family of Jerusalem formed marriage alliances with the house of Samaria, in defiance of Ezra and Nehemiah's marriage laws—the schism between Samaritans and Judeans of Jerusalem occurred only later. Nabatean tribal leaders established themselves in Transjordan and North Arabia and did not come under state control until annexed by the Romans in the second century c.e. Trade to the west with Greece continued, and the Persians hired mercenaries from their old enemy Athens to fight their campaigns. Nevertheless Greece did not move in to dominate Palestine until late in the fourth century, when Alexander of Macedon set out to conquer the Persian Empire.

12

Greek Rulers and Rome's Hasmoneans

With the conquests of Alexander the Great (336–323), the Greeks, who had entered the eastern Mediterranean scene previously among the "sea peoples" raiding the Egyptian Empire, then as city-state rivals to the Persians, as well as mercenaries in Egyptian, Babylonian, Philistine, Phoenician, Judean, and Persian service, took over the imperial role. Asia Minor fell in 333, Egypt in 332, Palestine in 331. Alexander's vast empire, however, stretching toward the world's wealth from Macedonia to India, soon fell apart along the fissure that runs, like an old crack under a new coat of paint, through Palestine, and the perennial contest between the Nile Valley and Mesopotamia over the eastern Mediterranean resumed, with the dynasty of Alexander's general Ptolemy representing Egypt and that of his general Seleucus in Syria representing Mesopotamia. The province of Judea fell first under the Ptolemies (312–200), then under the Seleucids (200–165).

Alexander and his successors introduced a Greek-based, cosmopolitan, hellenistic urban culture to the east. While people continued to speak Aramaic in Seleucid Syria and late Egyptian (eventually written in the Greek-based "Coptic" script) in Ptolemaic Egypt, Greek became the language of government, commerce, diplomacy, education, and prestige in the network of city-states that ruled the empire. In Palestine, where commercial and military traffic brought city and rural life close together, Aramaic eventually gave some ground to Greek as an urban language, and Judean culture developed a hellenistic facet. Judeans, many of whom prospered in Persian courts and cities, continued to thrive in increased numbers in Alexander's cities, though not always at peace with their neighbors. As more of them acquired the schooling that was the jewel of Greek culture, the priests lost their monopoly on access to the scriptures. By the middle of the third century, the main Hebrew temple scriptures had been translated into Greek, and possibly Aramaic as well.

Alexander's empire was ruled by cities built or rebuilt on the Greek model, governed by a city council loyal to the monarch. Alexandria, founded in 331 as the new capital of Egypt, and Antioch in Syria became the first megacities—megalopolises—of the empire, to be surpassed later only by Rome and Constantinople. Situated at points where the Nile Valley met and the Euphrates Valley closely approached the Mediterranean, they opened the Egyptian and coastal Syrian breadbaskets to the west, which soon depended on them for food, assuring their permanent importance. As the centers of population and trade, they also became the centers of learning: Alexandria's library was reputed the greatest in the ancient world.

Greek cities housed the amenities of Greek life: the agora, or open market and assembly place, the stoa, a collonaded market porch, baths, gymnasiums, stadiums, theaters, libraries, and temples, all breeding places for the mental and physical as well as economic development beloved of Greek urban culture. Scores of existing cities got new Greek names: thus Akko in Palestine became Ptolemais and Rabba in Ammon became Philadelphia, both in honor of the Egyptian ruling house. (Such Greek names were a veneer, however, and usually failed to stick.) Temples at the center of city life ran cults of indigenous deities under Greek names (Baal as Zeus, for example) or imported Greek cults. Beyond the cities, the Greeks maintained the Persian system of satrapies and provinces. Judeans quickly made their way to the cities and in the greatest of them became numerous. In time Judeans made up the majority of residents, for example, in two of Alexandria's five districts.

Many of the governors of Alexander's empire, once his military commanders, came from the farming class in Greece. They combined, therefore, an expertise in agricultural technology previous elites had lacked with the usual interest in greater production. Aided by orderly imperial administration, they presided over a boom in agricultural production. Throughout the empire, rulers and temples bulged with food and loot.

In Palestine the Greeks ruled through local strongmen, who commanded their own garrisons of mercenaries recruited from as far away as Athens and Macedonia. The subject populations, likewise a mix of local and resettled people, worked on great estates supporting the cities where the landowners lived. An increasing number of the workers were slaves, slavery being an Athenian institution widespread in the empire. Huge supplies of grain accumulated in the cities, little of it reaching the growing rural population that raised it.

During this period the possibilities latent in a simple alphabet were at last realized in the spread of literacy called by some the literate revolution. In the hellenistic urban world created by the pupil of Aristotle the student of Plato and Socrates, learning became prestigious. Judean scribes, now the bearers of literacy for their people in the Greek world, were influenced by Greek intellectual trends, even while they continued to write in Hebrew and Aramaic. The book of Ecclesiastes, though Semitic in diction and rhetoric, was composed under the influence of Greek commercial culture and the school of Skepticism. The Platonist idealism long popular in Alexandria was adopted by the Judean philosopher Philo in the first century C.E. and other Judean and Christian thinkers still later. As the ability to read and thus to interpret scripture spread, the Torah and other temple scriptures translated into Greek during the reign of Ptolemy II (283–246) tended to become fixed texts, resistant to further revision.

The first Greek translations of the scriptures were made for use by Judeans outside Palestine, who formed associations for worship and study in the districts where they lived. By this time many passages in the scriptures were no longer understood, due to poor texts or changes in Hebrew, but when the translators were stumped they made a more or less intelligent guess as to meaning, as translators still do. Under Ptolemy III (246–221) signs appear of the synagogue, often a leader's home, where the study of the Judean scriptures was furthered and Judean prayer services held. Within three centuries, synagogues would replace the temple as the center of Judean cultic life. (In defiance of Josiah's law, alternative temples were also built, in Egypt, Samaria, and elsewhere.) Though Greek in name, the synagogue was not a purely hellenistic institution, as the Greeks kept cult and schooling separate. Synagogue assemblies copied voluntary associations of votaries in Ptolemaic Egypt, like those of Isis and Serapis, and a similar combination of worship and learning can be seen in the "house of life," a library and study room attached to many Egyptian temples. As families found themselves uprooted and relocated in the empire's cities, district-based voluntary associations provided networks of affiliation for a mobile population.

Ptolemaic Egypt extended as far as New Kingdom Egypt had, but before long maintained itself only with Roman support. By the early second century, following Rome's victories against Carthage in the Punic wars, Egypt had fallen under the control of Rome, which from then on fed its population on Egyptian grain (and homegrown circuses). The Ptolemies ruled as Roman puppets until the dynasty ended with lovelorn Cleopatra's death in 30 B.C.E.

The Ptolemies governed the Judean community through the temple, granting privileges to the Aaronid priesthood that administered the temple laws. Unlike the Persians, the Ptolemies did not appoint civil governors parallel to the high priests, although they did spread their tax concessions among other priestly and nonpriestly families. The priests, therefore, as major landholders, became the exclusive legal authorities in the land. However, through the old, once subversive connection established in the Persian period between the priestly landholders and the imperial cities, the Ptolemies were able to exercise control over the Aaronids and influence the choice of high priest within the dynastic succession. The Seleucids meanwhile fished for support among the magnates, exploiting family rivalries like the longstanding hostility between the high priestly Oniads and the Tobiads, a family whose political clout dated from Nehemiah's time, and wooing them with offers of greater economic and legal privileges.

Pressured by Persia's new Parthian rulers, by the mid-third century the Seleucid sector of Alexander's empire had begun to shrink. By the mid-second century it was to be reduced to parts of Syria and Cilicia (south-central Turkey). The Seleucid king Antiochus III (223–187) cast his eye toward Egypt, and on the accession of five-year-old Ptolemy V took Palestine from Rome's ward. (The first anniversary of this same Ptolemy's coronation ten years later was commemorated by the Rosetta Stone seized during Napoleon's invasion of Egypt; written in hieroglyphic Egyptian, demotic Egyptian, and Greek, it provided the key to deciphering Egyptian and launched the rediscovery of the ancient Near East.) Antiochus's policy toward Judea was at first conciliatory: to confirm the new regime in Jerusalem he issued an official letter, or charter, providing material for the temple's buildings and sacrifices, and declaring that Judeans should have a form of government in accord with its laws and that the council of elders, priests, and scribes of the temple, and the temple singers the Levites, should be relieved of poll tax. He reconfirmed the purity of the temple, which was closed to non-Judeans and unclean Judeans, and the validity of the dietary laws supervised by priests.

Antiochus's imperial ambitions toward Persia and the west were checked by the Romans, who by the Treaty of Apamea in 188 imposed a heavy annual indemnity on Seleucid Syria and forced Antiochus to reduce his navy, slaughter his elephants, and send his second son to Rome as a hostage. Thereafter the Romans regularly kept an alternative claimant to the throne, from one branch or the other of the ruling family, in reserve. Having lost most of his income with the loss of his ships in the Mediterranean and his land in Greece and Asia Minor, Antiochus turned to the well-endowed temples of his realm to supply his need. After his death following a temple raid in 187, his successors carried on the policy. Relations with Judea deteriorated.

The book of Ecclesiasticus (not to be confused with Ecclesiastes), containing the sayings of Ben Sira, dates from the era of Antiochus III. Ben Sira was a temple scribe under the high priest Simon II of the Oniads, supporters of Antiochus III. "Fear the Lord and honor the priest," he urges. His collected proverbs express court values, that is, the value of hard work by people ordained to do it, not scribes who need leisure to fulfill their peculiar destiny, and temple values: "a merchant can hardly avoid wrongdoing and a tradesman will not be exonerated from sin." Aaron, Phineas, Zadok, Onias III, and Simon II (Ecclus. 50:1-26), the hereditary Aaronid priesthood, are hailed as embodiments of wisdom. The collection was written about 190 and translated into Greek two generations later in Egypt, where Onias IV, by then a general in the Ptolemaic army, had built a temple in exile at Leontopolis. The Hebrew original was not known until the discovery of manuscript fragments from the sixth to ninth centuries C.E. discarded in the Cairo geniza, the rubbish room of a Cairo synagogue, in the late nineteenth century.

Seleucid rule in Palestine foundered on Rome's policy—the exorbitant demand for tribute and the rivalry fostered by Rome among members of the ruling family—as well as on competition with Egypt. Antiochus's successors again turned to robbing temples for tribute money. The high priest Onias III protested in vain to Antiochus's successor Seleucus that the temple treasury, fed by funds bequeathed to it in return for tax relief, was designated to support the widows and fatherless children of the donors. (Eventually the Christian churches adopted a version of this temple function, while Judean communities maintained the practice of almsgiving.)

Antiochus III's second son, Antiochus IV, an enthusiastic hellenophile who had been in Rome's hostage bullpen before succeeding to the throne at his brother's death, thought to secure tribute money and his Egyptian border by selling the position of high priest in Jerusalem to the highest bidder, thus removing it from the Aaronid family for the first time in at least three hundred, if not eight hundred, years. His first appointee, Jason, an Oniad (but note his Greek name), undertook to hellenize the city with the introduction of Greek costume and customs, like a new gymnasium. Under the next, a non-Aaronid named Menelaus, Antiochus indulged in robbing and massacring in Jerusalem and a plan to dedicate the temple to his favorite god, Olympian Zeus. After a disastrous attempt to invade Egypt in 168, during which the Roman general in Egypt repulsed him in humiliation, he abrogated the temple law and desecrated the temple altar in some manner too obscene to name, referred to in the book of Daniel as the "abomination of desolation." Judeans were forbidden to keep the Sabbath or practice circumcision and were forced to violate dietary and other purity laws.

Organized resistance to the Seleucid attempt to make Palestine a militarized zone under martial law and direct imperial control as a buffer against Egypt (as Rome will make it against Parthia) went on for three years (167–164). One scriptural document from this war, the book of Daniel, argued that the right response to Antiochus's depredations was to wait patiently for God's deliverance and suffer martyrdom if necessary, as Seleucid power was to be broken "by no human hand" (Dan. 8:25). But popular feeling—in some factions evoked by the patron's word—favored taking matters into Judean hands. With Roman encouragement, a guerrilla gang led by descendants of Hasmon, Matthias and his three sons, including Judas the Hammer (Hebrew *maqqab*), grasped the opportunity to create an autonomous domain. Later assuming the titles of high priest and then king, the Hasmoneans, or Maccabees, ended up ruling a kingdom sometimes larger than Solomon's for more than a hundred years. Each succeeding Maccabee compacted with Rome, formally or informally, to make trouble for the Seleucids, whom the Romans did not formally overthrow for another century. Like David, the Maccabees conquered their kingdom in the name of Judean independence but in fact as hellenistic princes governed by the imperial rules of the day.

In 164 the Maccabees captured Jerusalem and refounded the temple, reinstating temple law. This event is commemorated in the feast of Hannukah, or (re)founding. Their victory and restoration of the law saved the temple scriptures in Jerusalem from oblivion at the hands of Antiochus, though they would have survived in Egypt, Babylonia, and elsewhere, probably to be regarded by modern scholars as mere antique curiosities. The author of Daniel, despite his pacifist message, served as the prophet of the Maccabees' success, having predicted Antiochus's fall and advocated passive subordination to authority.

Hostile to the Seleucid appointees who had discredited the high priesthood by their dealings, the Maccabees appointed their own priests to supervise the use of temple law as the law of their rule. The Seleucids, however, retained a nominal right to dispose of the high priesthood and continued to use the offer to engage support. Seven years after the high priest Alcimus, a Seleucid appointee and the last of the Aaronids, died because he tore down a temple wall (as Maccabean propaganda had it), the Hasmonean family, priests of a minor non-Aaronid branch, filled the vacancy themselves in the person of Judas's successor Jonathan. Roles had reversed: now the two contending branches of Seleucids let loose by Rome on Syria and Palestine were induced to bid against each other for the services of the Maccabees, with the high priesthood the Maccabean prize, endorsed, quite contrary to temple law, by a "great assembly" of picked priests and chiefs. From then on the Maccabees grew in strength by playing Rome's hand, pitting Seleucid against Seleucid. In 142 the reigning Seleucid granted autonomy to the temple and Hasmonean high priest, now brother Simon, officially relinquishing the jurisdiction lost in reality twenty years earlier. The merging of high priestly and royal prerogatives was complete, though the royal title lay in abeyance for another generation.

The Hasmonean era saw important changes in the makeup of the priesthood. Initially the Aaronids, whose supremacy dated from before the Persians, dominated the temple with their administrative assistants the Levites, while in the country at large shadowy hasidim practiced their brand of piety and purity. In place of the discredited Zadokite Aaronids, Judas appointed a new class, who took the name of the Zadokites (in Greek: Sadducees) and, piggybacking on the Hasmoneans, soon increased in numbers and wealth. The displaced Aaronids faded into obscurity with the faction of Alcimus or followed their leader Onias IV into Egypt, where they built their rival temple. Some went to the country with hasidim and formed a cult community at Qumran on the Dead Sea and at other localities, where they awaited God's war to bring about their restoration to power in a restored temple. The "righteous teacher" mentioned in their documents seems to have been an Aaronid priest with hasidic tendencies who broke with the Maccabees under the usurping "wicked priest," Jonathan or Simon. This group, the Essenes, kept and copied the temple scriptures (possibly excepting Esther) and produced the Dead Sea scrolls discovered in 1947 and later, the oldest copies of the temple scriptures known.

After the Aaronids, the administration of temple law among the people fell into the hands of scholars and adjudicators called pharisees, whose name, possibly invented by opponents, means "sectaries" or "party men," "separated" from priestly interpretation of temple law. The historian Josephus mentions them first at this point, when the factionalized, venal, pro-Seleucid high priesthood fell into disrepute. In time the pharisees achieved a corner on practical legal interpretation, as well as sharing with the hasidim rigorous observation of the piety of purity, in reaction to the laxity they observed in an increasing number of Judean elite.

At first the pharisees supported the Hasmoneans, who regarded all such quasi-priestly groups, including Alcimus's faction of compliant Aaronids, as law-abiding hasidim. Pharisees may have joined the "great assembly" that confirmed Jonathan to the high priesthood in 152. Afterward, though, many became uneasy about the Maccabean tendency to subordinate the high priesthood to the royal authority of their joint position. Conflict with the Maccabees' Sadducean priesthood over local jurisdiction in Palestine consolidated the pharisees' sense that their identity and their right to apply the law stemmed from their fidelity to the scriptures. They were not to become rulers, however, until under the name rabbis they were confirmed in their role by the Romans in the third century C.E. (only to be spurned two centuries later).

Unlike the Hasmonean wealthy, landowning temple priesthood, the pharisees came from the craft and artisan class, transformed by the addition of learning. They regarded the temple's laws as the basis not only for the piety practiced in their men-only dinner clubs, associations for observance of the food and purity laws, but for the practice of useful arts as well, including agriculture, by which the food for their dinners was produced, a notion intimated already in P. Though they shared with equally learned temple scribes responsibility for applying the ancestral law among the people, they diverged from the temple scribes' view of the law as enshrined in written texts whose permanence they were bound to conserve in an age of spreading literacy. This the scribes did by promoting wisdom as the rational discernment of right action in prudence, leaving the revealed law alone—a concept put forth, for instance, by Ben Sira. In contrast, the pharisees, spiritual kin to hellenistic Cynics, said wisdom lay in the process of discovering the meaning of torah, practicing it, and presenting it orally. Sensitive to the injustice often rigidified by the written text, and lacking the scribes' direct connection with the temple repository of written law, they chose not to record their law, but to emphasize the prerogative of oral as equivalent to written law.

In so doing they adopted the dialectic process deriving from Socrates and Plato and popular in contemporary hellenistic philosophical theory. Traces of their style of teaching, said to have been done in dialectic pairs, appear in the Mishnah, where the recorded discussions, unlike Plato's, rarely result in a definitive ruling. Against the background of the increasing popularity, especially in the first century C.E., of the Stoics' authoritarian philosophy, the pharisees sympathized with the Cynic tradition that held that way of life, praxis, was more important than abstract theory. When Josephus equated pharisees with Stoics, he was thinking of establishment, cosmopolitan, royalist pharisees like himself, not the rural, largely landless, pious teachers for whom contemporary legal systems represented unjust convention codified.

Though the Hasmoneans ruled Judea first by right of holding the high priesthood, they increasingly assumed the royal prerogatives appropriate to their power and autonomy—and gave their sons Greek names. John Hyrcanus (134–104), who revived the practice of hiring Greek mercenaries for his troops, was the first Judean ruler to mint his own coins. With his son he created a commercial empire larger and wealthier than Solomon's based in the growing power of Rome. Backed by the new priestly elite, the Sadducees, he pursued an antipharisee hellenizing policy. The Maccabees had fueled antihellenistic feeling inspired by Antiochus's atrocities to launch themselves as rulers in the name of temple law, but in the second generation they were no more anti-Greek than Solomon was anti-Canaanite. John's son Alexander Jannaeus (103-76) claimed the title of king when he succeeded to the high priesthood. During his reign a civil war raged for five years, in which eight hundred pharisees, who had asked for Seleucid support, were crucified. Alexander arranged for his widow, Salome Alexandra, to inherit the crown, but the high priesthood, not being open to women, went to her son. Thus for the first time since the Persians, secular rule was detached from high priestly rule, as it continued to be under the Romans.

Conflict between Alexander's two sons, one Hyrcanus the high priest, the other Aristobolus, backed by an Idumean bedouin sheikh called Antipater, plagued the last years of Hasmonean rule and even led Salome to reinstate the once-persecuted pharisees, who were perhaps more tolerant of a woman ruler than the Sadducees were. Hyrcanus eventually appealed to Rome against his brother's claims. Pompey, the Roman commander in the east, responded by capturing Jerusalem in 63, seizing Hasmonean royal lands and those of Judean resisters, and liberating the Greek cities in Palestine from unpopular Judean rule. His desecration of the temple resulted in the Psalms of Solomon in the Apocrypha. With Hyrcanus under Roman hegemony as high priest and *ethnarchos* (head of "nation") over Judea—an appointment later confirmed by Julius Caesar and other Roman rulers—but not as king, the Hasmonean dynasty came to an end. Aristobolus was banished to Rome.

Legitimation documents for the Hasmonean regime and its new priesthood entered the scriptures as 1 and 2 Maccabees, 2 Maccabees from the earlier reign of John Hyrcanus and 1 Maccabees from Alexander Jannaeus's reign. The original 1 Maccabees, now lost, was written in Hebrew in an archaizing style imitating Ezra, Nehemiah, and Chronicles. In an effort to counter their Greek image, Hasmonean scribes used Hebrew in place of Aramaic and revived the use of the archaic Hebrew script of the monarchic period. This Hebrew script, which must have been recovered from ancient temple documents, was soon abandoned again, to survive as the script of anti-Hasmonean Samaritans, who at this time first achieved their distinct identity in the north and elsewhere in the Mediterranean world.

First Maccabees is a history of the sons of Matthias, Judas and his brothers, up to the murder of Simon, and thus the history of the founding of the dynasty. Like David's apologia for the overthrow of the Saulids, the document justifies the usurpation of the high priesthood from the Aaronids. It claims legitimation first on the basis of their deeds: the Hasmoneans fought "for the law and the sanctuary" with a zeal to match that of Phineas the son of Aaron. Judas is presented as a temple builder. Moreover Palestine's overlords approved them. From Jonathan's elevation in 152 on, every succeeding Seleucid ruler confirmed the Hasmonean appointment. The Romans too had first agreed to stop the installation of Alcimus and then confirmed both Jonathan and Simon in their positions. Popular acclaim by "the people of Jerusalem" in the great assembly of 152 was adduced. God's approval, anticipated by Daniel's prophecy, was evident from the Maccabees' success and clinched the matter. The Maccabees have the right "to be clothed in purple and to wear gold," and to be strong militarily (despite Daniel). First Maccabees deals with Aaronid opposition by ignoring it, the brief references to Alcimus being the only mention of opposing high priests.

Second Maccabees, presented as an epitome of a much longer history in Greek, focuses on the temple itself. It deals in detail with the high priests Onias, Simon, Jason, and Menelaus, and ends with the Seleucid general Nicanor, whose death sealed Judas Maccabee's control of Jerusalem and the temple. Judas's exploits in defense of the temple and Judean people are recounted. A dream in which Onias requests that Judas receive a golden sword from the saint Jeremiah symbolizes the transfer of power from the Aaronids to the Hasmoneans.

The book of Judith, also written at this time, possibly following a folk model, celebrated the defense of Judean heartland against the imperial enemy in the name of the Judean people. Written in Greek for court use, it is an example of a patriarchal fairy tale about the extraordinary power of the weak (women) to overthrow the strong.

13

Roman Rulers, Herodians, and the End of the Temple

In making the Mediterranean a Roman lake and hammering together the greatest empire the world would know for fifteen hundred years, Rome reset the geopolitical pattern of the Near East. The old rivalry between the Nile and Mesopotamia was engulfed in a wider west-east contest between Rome and Persia (Parthians until the third century, then Sasanians), with Palestine always a border area to the southwest of the main arena of conflict. Under the auspices of the so-called Roman peace, Palestine became one of the militarized peripheral zones governed directly by the emperor and his appointees. Though the Judean state lingered in nominal existence until it became a Roman province in 70 C.E., Roman rule in Palestine was set to endure for the rest of the biblical period.

In Hyrcanus's Judea real power lay with Antipater, the Idumean sheikh, who fought for Julius Caesar in Egypt and in return was made procurator (Roman governor) of Judea. His son Herod, reputed among the Romans as a forceful gang leader ready to flout the priesthood's jurisdiction, managed to climb the Roman ladder from governor of Galilee, then of Syria as well, to tetrarch of Palestine, and finally to appointment as "king of the Judeans." He stayed on the merry-go-round of power set whirling by Julius Caesar's assassination, until Antony won the kingship for him in order to oust Hyrcanus's nephew from Jerusalem and throw back an invasion by the Hasmonean's Parthian backers. With a Roman army supplied by Antony, Herod recaptured Jerusalem in 37 B.C.E. and reigned as king until his death in 4 B.C.E.

Throughout a long and energetic reign Herod never quite succeeded in establishing the legitimacy of his rule beyond his Roman backing. He himself could not be high priest because he was not of a priestly family and Judean only through his mother. He destroyed the authority of the existing high priestly class and failed to create a credible substitute for it. Potential challenge from the deposed Hasmoneans he met in two ways: murder and marriage. He murdered forty-five members of the sanhedrin sympathetic with the Hasmoneans. Then he married Mariamne, a granddaughter of Hyrcanus, and had his brother and son marry Hasmonean women as well. Murder prevailed over marriage: Herod drowned a brother of Mariamne after making him high priest (he proved too popular), executed Hyrcanus, and had two of his own sons by Mariamne strangled.

Herod chose to undercut local authority by recruiting a foreign ruling class. His closest adviser was a Spartan, his army commanders mostly Greek and Roman. The few Judean officers he used were from the wealthy Judean community of Babylonia, as were the tutors employed in his family. For high priests, he brought in prestigious Alexandrian and Babylonian Judeans, possibly with priestly credentials but with few if any connections in Palestinian networks, and allowed them as individuals only brief terms in office. Seven high priests served in his thirty-three-year reign, one (the sole likely Palestinian) for a day. The high priest Boethus, one of Herod's fathers-in-law, however, lasted from 24 to 5 B.C.E.

Like all proper rulers, Herod made his authority visible in a building program. He founded cities, the most important being Caesarea, the new port on the coast, which quickly established itself as the capital of Roman administration in Palestine and an impressive Greco-Roman city in a region lacking in them. To suppress tribes and brigands in his realm and defend against personal enemies, he had fortress palaces built, several in desert locales. The palace in Jerusalem, built in 23 B.C.E., occupied twenty thousand square yards and could accommodate fifteen hundred people at a time. Herod's masons were fond of huge ashlar blocks, still seen at the Herodian sites which along with Crusader sites dominate the visible antiquities of Palestine.

Part of his massive building program was a reconstruction of the temple in Jerusalem begun about 18 B.C.E. on such a massive scale that it was not finished until 64 C.E. The project was financed by Herod himself and by contributions from wealthy Judeans outside of Palestine. A colossal platform was prepared, still extant as the massive platform of the Dome of the Rock, whose southwest wall forms today's Wailing Wall. This temple, a far cry from David's private tent, was a wonder of the eastern world. Thirty-five acres of arches, gates, porticoes, balustrades, stairways, pools, waterworks, and buildings, with foundations nearly a mile around, it was one of the largest construction projects in the history of the Roman empire—and new home for the temple scriptures. Herod refurbished the site of the tomb of Abraham at the Cave of Machpelah in Hebron, in his Idumean father's territory, with another gigantic construction.

For the grander temple the Levitical temple service was expanded by the addition of most of Psalms 90–150 (many date to earlier times), and more—the exact number of official psalms was not set until after the destruction of the temple. The new construction inspired the collection of "psalms of the steps" (Pss. 120–134), composed or revised on the basis of the blessing of Aaron in Numbers 6:22-27—a nice allusion to Aaronid memory. One psalm was to be recited in procession on each of the steps leading to the temple's inner court. The concluding psalm of the present collection (Ps. 150) evoked the grandeur of the temple's festival music under the opulence of the Herodian regime. This expansion of Psalms was the only scripture affected by Herod's seizure of power.

At Herod's death the Judeans petitioned to have Herodian rule discontinued. The emperor Augustus, however, upheld Herod's will that his kingdom be divided among three sons he hadn't murdered (the Romans continued to hold rival claimants in reserve). Judea, Samaria, and Idumea went to Archelaus (to 6 C.E.), Galilee and Perea just east of the Jordan to Herod Antipas (to 39 C.E.), and northern Transjordanian districts to Philip (to 34 C.E.). On complaint from both Judeans and Samaritans, after a decade the Romans deposed Archelaus, who suffered not only from his brothers' intrigues but from association with a losing faction in the imperial court, and thereafter ruled directly through procurators.

Antipas ruled his sector of the realm for more than forty years. He drafted labor to build a city on the Sea of Galilee, named Tiberias in honor of the second emperor, Tiberius. He faced little direct resistance during his reign, but when he asked to be made king was set aside by Emperor Caligula, who preferred a rival in an inter-Herodian struggle. Philip's subjects were mostly non-Judean. He enlarged Caesarea Philippi north of the Sea of Galilee into a Greco-Roman city.

Herod the Great's divided realm was reunited under his grandson Herod Agrippa (named for a friend and general of Augustus), the only successor in Herod's line to wield anything like Herod's power. Herod had killed Agrippa's father and sent Agrippa himself to Rome, where he became a protégé of Caligula. Caligula appointed him to Philip's post on Philip's death and then removed Antipas to Gaul in Agrippa's favor; Emperor Claudius added Samaria and Judea to his domain. Another builder, Agrippa undertook to enlarge and strengthen the walls of Jerusalem. Though he continued Herod's policy of looking for support to non-Palestinian Judeans, he cultivated popularity by patronizing local groups like the pharisees.

Agrippa's short reign (41–44) was the only break in the direct rule by procurators who governed Judea and Samaria from 6 to 41 and Judea, Samaria, and Galilee from 44 to 66. Several of these are named in the New Testament: Pontius Pilate (26–36), Felix (52–60), and Festus (60–62). Agrippa's son Agrippa II held a tetrarchy in Chalcis, probably in northern Syria, with authority in the jurisdiction of the temple in Jerusalem, from 48 to the mid-50s. He and his sister Berenice went to Rome after the fall of Jerusalem as intimate friends of the victorious general Titus. When Titus became emperor in 79, however, he sent her back to Judea.

The Herodian Judean elite amassed their wealth in the traditional way: they creamed taxes and acquired lands as gifts from the rulers or through foreclosure on debt. Hard times fell on the villagers as in the days of the Omrids. Urban troubles exacerbated rural ones. When the temple was finished in 64, the huge work force thus thrown out of work was set to paving Jerusalem in marble, to keep them from joining the unruly rabble. Judea was infested with the indigent, in the cities and in the countryside. While the Romans had no patience with the destitute, Judean custom, later continued by both Jews and Christians, cared for them, if only to keep them just above starvation. With traditional networks of support and discipline frayed, banditry became endemic from the 40s on: an Eleazar led a gang in the hills leading up to Jerusalem, a Jesus operated in Galilee in 66–67, with close ties to urban Sepphoris. Outside Palestine, synagogues were becoming centers of community discipline, but before 70 synagogues in Palestine probably could not fulfill this role.

In Palestine like everywhere else, Roman administration was expected to preserve law and order and to collect taxes. Generally the Romans were able to rely on local men of good birth, morals, and wealth to do this for them. The elite created by Herod, however, proved a poor instrument of local leadership because despite its wealth and power, it lacked authority and prestige. Herod's officers' Roman ties discredited them with the people, and they had few local ties.

Rome was baffled by the high priests and their like, who had no Roman education or military training, rarely achieved Roman citizenship, and never aspired to the Roman senate. Efforts to manipulate the high priesthood, now definitively sundered from the office of king, faltered. Joazar of Boethus's priestly family, appointed by Rome in 6 C.E. to organize the census, aroused such widespread resistance led by Judah the Galilean (the beginnings of the Galilee gang of the 60s) that he had to be replaced immediately, and the family did not come back to power as high priests again until Agrippa I. Eventually Rome appointed Ananus son of Sethi, whose family dominated the high priesthood as Roman puppets until the destruction of the temple; he was high priest for nine years, followed by five of his sons.

In the later Herodian period the temple priesthood, the bailiwick of four or five families all known collectively as "high priests," fell completely into the hands of the Roman governors and their puppets, the Herodian princes. Only Agrippa I retained some autonomy in making the appointments. From 6 on, the high priest's garments were kept by the king or procurator. High priests continued to flit in and out of office, without benefit of the traditional confirmation by the popular assembly: Agrippa made six changes between 57 and 66. The revolving-door priests had no authority with the people. They needed instruction in the rites, they controlled little or no land (the temple had little), and they had no access to temple funds, which like appointments were controlled by the procurators and after 44 by Herodian princes.

Herod and Archelaus tended to select their least influential, non-Judean courtiers for the priesthood. Rome confounded their difficulties by suppressing the popular assembly that could have given these priestly families some legitimacy, because Rome always preferred to rule through an oligarchy of rich, rather than through the assemblies of Greek and other traditions. The crowd did have influence, however, often sending embassies to the Romans or presenting their petitions directly. The sanhedrin (from a Greek word meaning "council"), often thought of as a representative assembly, was simply the advisory council of the incumbent high priest, consisting of his circle of priestly supporters, plus the odd legal expert, possibly a pharisee or two. This council assisted the high priest as a tribunal in those areas of jurisdiction Rome was willing to leave to the temple. Its members were the council of chief tax collectors for Rome, but they often had difficulty fulfilling this essential function in the increasing anarchy of 6–66.

Herod had created a great new building to house the temple scriptures, but undercut the jurisdiction of the scriptures' guardians, the temple priesthood. During and after his reign others moved in to fill the void, interpreting and preserving the meaning of the scriptures for Judeans. In the first century C.E., village courts and relations among workers began to be influenced by the associations of self-announced interpreters of the law, the pharisees, scribes, Essenes, and the occasional outlaw and saint, who proliferated in the land and whose authority was based on legal learning and subtlety, qualities the official rich priesthood lacked.

Prominent among these were the pharisees, who emerged as we have seen in the Hasmonean period. The Essenes also stemmed from that time. The ruling class spawned a group of wealthy Sadducees, not necessarily the same Sadducees who formed the Hasmonean priesthood, who accepted only the Torah as authoritative. Cushioned by riches, they rejected the prophets' divans, the pharisees' oral law, and belief in an afterlife and saints and other intermediaries. The Levites continued to work in the temple service and guard the scriptures, and probably supplied many of the scribes of the period. Eventually the scribes hived off from the Levites and, benefiting from the decline in priestly authority and from the growth of literacy under Hellenistic influence, spread throughout the culture, often attached to the pharisees. These groups were not mutually exclusive; an individual might bear several of these labels and play several roles.

The pharisees were tolerated by Herod the Great and other Roman rulers because as fatalists they did not call for armed rebellion against the occupation, and in practice they were useful for keeping law and order. The spread of synagogues in the face of the temple's decline in authority was another arena of their growing influence.

Placing a high value on education and scholarly pursuits, they scorned the pursuit of wealth practiced by the Herodian priestly elite, though their system of purity did not enjoin poverty (in this respect differing from Cynics, whose teaching and preaching technique otherwise influenced many pharisees). They were extravagantly jealous of their popularity and mostly self-assigned jurisdictional prerogatives. The most famous pharisees of the Herodian period were Shammai, his sparring partner Hillel, and the latter's descendants Gamaliel and Simeon. Hillel belonged to a Babylonian family richer than that of the average pharisee, which survived the fall of Jerusalem to become important in subsequent rabbinic history.

Some of the law's new interpreters sought to throw off the forms of culture and live an ascetic life in the wilderness, awaiting the coming of God in judgment. They formed lodges similar to Elisha's in the reign of the Omrids, and for much the same reasons. One such ascetic, John the Immerser (Baptizer), practiced in the southern portion of Antipas's territory, across the Jordan from Jericho. Many thought that in the tradition of local saints John, who resembled Elijah, must represent the return of Elijah that the book of Malachi said portended God's war of judgment. John purified all comers in the Jordan River at the spot where Elijah was last seen, snatched alive into the sky, and where the Judean people had traditionally recapitulated the escape from bondage in Egypt that had created them a nation dedicated to social justice. John denounced Antipas's marriage to his sister-in-law Herodias, whom Antipas grew fond of while on a visit to Rome, and Antipas took this as an excuse to have him beheaded.

Pharisee and ascetic, teacher and saint, came together, probably not for the first time, in the person of Jeshua of Nazareth in Galilee (Hebrew: Joshua; Greek: Jesus), possibly in his day called *messiah* or, in the Greek of his followers' later urban assemblies, *christos*, "anointed one, seditionist." Jesus was an artisan who received training as a pharisee and from John the Baptizer, and in the reign of Tiberius and governorship of Pontius Pilate returned to Galilee with practices and a message that attracted a following. In the tradition of the saints he tried to find ways of bridging the gap between the ruling class of richer landowners and the poor. He healed the ill, lame, and demonized, and presented himself as the harbinger and arbiter of God's rule, when society's fundamentally unjust order would be overturned. His labor of feeding, healing, and teaching he regarded as sufficient to embody God's new order, devoid for the present of any trace of force or coercion and hence open-ended in its political direction.

Jesus worked mainly among Judeans in Galilee and adjacent lands, where he taught in Aramaic and perhaps Hebrew. He visited both rural and cosmopolitan areas, but shunned the Greek cities like Sepphoris and Tiberias. Despite this conservatism, his concept of the law required that the scriptures be bent to serve the needs of people in the field. He was as prepared as the next pharisee to face poverty if necessary and persecution for his threatening views. He distinguished himself, however, from the pharisaic fellowship by his inclusive disregard for the rules of purity, which gave the pharisees difficulty in regarding him as one of their own. He shared the pharisees' Cynical assumptions as regarded oral law, but carried them further, dispensing with the fellowship in purity of the pharisaic eating clubs and creating his own fellowship to demonstrate God's new order based on unqualified forgiving and forgoing of self-righteousness.

Jesus' pharisaic aversion to recorded wisdom left his teaching open to various interpretations. The indirection of his speech, influenced by wisdom, also created ambiguity; his teaching's multivalency may have been due to avoiding political risks, although Jesus did not shy from confrontation, at least with Judeans, and ultimately with Rome's governor. Thus Jesus' defiance of the purity laws left his followers free to receive non-Judeans into their fellowship, even if Jesus himself had not sought them out, since the ritual definition of Judean identity itself seemed to be under attack. Many followers, however, were reluctant to go so far. His teaching also lent itself to apocalyptic interpretation, as under prevailing circumstances there could be no doubt to anyone who knew the scriptures that God would create the new order through war. Teachings by and about Jesus soon were called *bishara*, "war report" (Greek: *euangelion*, translated "gospel").

Jesus led followers to Jerusalem, the venue for God's overthrow of injustice. Though Jesus expected the temple to be purified in the process, undoubtedly he, like Isaiah, regarded it as God's permanent capital and lighthouse. His following was now spread in Galilee, Perea, Jerusalem, and elsewhere, attracting notice and requiring an official response, even though, as far as the evidence indicates, Jesus taught nothing against Herod or the Romans, but focused his pharisaic attention exclusively on the constitution of the new Judean nation. Again as in Isaiah, all else would follow in God's own time. While not a rebel, he added his wile to peasant protest and resistance. In Jerusalem he was executed by Pilate, known to be vicious, apparently as a pretender to the throne—an outlandish charge for such a vagabond, and a charge whose political implications were not taken up by his followers. This event like scores of similar executions went virtually unnoticed at the time.

Jesus' followers, including members of his family, were reluctant to accept their leader's death as a permanent setback. They stayed in Jerusalem as a cult group attending at his tomb. When Jesus was seen and heard again there, as heroes and saints often were near their grave sites, his appearance confirmed that his forecast of God's rule was true and that he himself would return at the culmination of the impending war to effect God's rule as God's anointed. In the meantime the fellowship, organized in assemblies, or cells (later in Greek *ekklesia*, to distinguish from *synagoge* with similar meaning; translated "church"), must bide their time, guided by the dynastic executive run by Jesus' brother Jacob (James), the new interim head of "Israel," with their office near the temple. They were to practice the rites of their cult, variants of Judean practices: a ritual immersion on admission, and a cult meal focused on the deceased hero, understood to have been instituted by Jesus himself. In time this immersion and meal came to replace the Judean rites of ritual bathing and Passover.

Leadership among the dispersed assemblies devolved upon the Twelve reputed to have enjoyed Jesus' intimate confidence during his life, a further embodiment of the new Israel. Before long there were too many assemblies and too few such apostles, and groups came under the direction of overseers (*paqid*; Greek: *episkopos*, "bishop"). These overseers administered the assemblies' self-help funds, contributed by followers (especially women) and probably kept on deposit in the temple like the national treasury and other private charitable endowments.

The assemblies met in and by the temple, and in synagogues, where people gathered to worship outside the confines of the temple and its scriptures. They attracted Greeks and other Greek speakers (gentiles) to the cult of the reseen Jesus expected to return to adjudicate in God's just rule. At the same time the cult spread to Caesarea and other urban centers of Judean population outside of Palestine, including Antioch, Alexandria, and other great cities, especially in the Roman Empire but also in the Persian Empire.

The cells were at first supposed to be run from mission control in Jerusalem, but because they quickly became wealthier and larger than the mother church they began to carry on their own affairs quite independent of Jerusalem. As voluntary associations for mutual support, not always based on family and patronage networks, the cells became increasingly intolerant of those outside the prescribed circle, whatever the circle was for a given cell—an intolerance that much later recommended them to imperial favor. After a generation or two they adopted the organizational forms of Roman society, especially the patriarchal household. The role of women then diminished from what it had been in the early decades of assemblies, when women were patrons of house cells and cell leaders, though an order of widows lasted for several centuries.

As the sect outgrew its Judean bounds, its widely inclusive interpretation of the law brought it into conflict with both the temple and the pharisees. The temple priesthood scoffed at theories about risen deceased and could dismiss the cult out of hand. Pharisees, themselves with saints in their past, saw nothing wrong in principle with the return of Jesus, but objected to the view that God's rule could be instigated by anything other than the prescribed purity of Israel, which Jesus failed to appreciate. Also, in their view, there was no need to venerate a deceased master as the continuing source of legal interpretation, since new masters were being continuously raised up, in God's wisdom, to take their place in ordered succession. (The cult of Jesus would have its succession, too, but not at the expense of Jesus' primacy.) Agrippa's persecution of James and Peter recounted in Acts may have resulted from his policy favoring the pharisees.

True to his pharisaic, Cynical character, Jesus did not, as far as is known, write anything. But those who came after him did, and the cells passed around numerous documents consisting of the deeds and words of the master and a growing number of letters dealing with matters of faith and order in the assemblies. The cells attempting to maintain contact among one another found travel and correspondence not difficult around the shores of the Roman lake. Some of these letters constitute the earliest documents in the New Testament. They were written by Saul (later Paul), one of the Christian (as they came to be called) organizers and speakers sent from eastern Judean centers to the urban world of the Roman Empire.

Paul came from an expatriate Judean family resident in Tarsus in southern Asia Minor. He became a pharisee and trained in Judea with the most prestigious teachers of his day. He was an artisan like most pharisees, but like few if any a Roman citizen, according to a late first-century narrator (Luke)—a most notable privilege. At first he shared pharisaic aversion to the cult of Jesus, but before long, on the basis of his own vision of the reseen lord, joined his followers.

This proved a significant addition to the organization. Paul was an energetic and learned rhetorician, grounded in both Judean and Greek traditions, legally privileged, a friend of wealthy, a promoter and organizer of the first order. He was deeply influenced by the Cynic elements in his training, and knew how to give intellectual respectability, in both Judean and Greek terms, to the suspension of the Judean torah—a law he regarded as in practice if not by nature divisive and oppressive—entailed in Jesus' resurrection. In the life and teachings of the Jesus who walked the ground in Palestine, Paul, not being a Palestinian Judean, took little interest. He was, however, convinced that the war anticipated by Jesus was imminent, and possessed a distinctive knack for depicting it in both terrifying and emboldening images.

Paul based himself in the Christian assembly in Antioch. From there he journeyed about in mid-century in Asia Minor and Greece and founded new cells in the major cities, whose prestige enhanced his career. He would go to a provincial or district capital, stay a few weeks, gather followers in the local synagogue and agora, and then leave the supervision of the new assemblies to local leadership. Four of his seven missionary years he spent in Corinth and Ephesus (busy port cities, the latter also a stimulating intellectual center), strategic localities that attracted streams of pilgrims to their famous cults. Judeans often showed at least some interest in the new cult, despite its strangeness, particularly because it was based in Jerusalem. For many the new ideas and practices answered to their alienation from surroundings and offered, like many eastern cults in the Roman world, an alternative and escape.

While at Ephesus Paul wrote 1 Corinthians and most of 2 Corinthians (a composite of letters) and Philemon, probably Galatians, and possibly Philippians. The letters to Corinth were designed to suppress the claim mooted there, especially among women, that possession of the baptismal spirit of Christ gave a person immediate resurrected and royal status, permitting them autonomy, or anarchy. Though many claimed Paul as their spiritual source, he rejected their right to disregard others, a hard response to hear from a man with his status and privileges. Philippians was a letter sent by Paul while incarcerated to thank the recipients for sending him a gift in prison (the right place from which to test rights and jurisdictions), which he takes as a token of the release of all from tribulation and therefore a source of joy. The letter to Philemon enjoined a slave-owner to take back his runaway slave without retribution, since statuses such as slave and master ought not to matter to Christians.

The same point—a two-edged sword as it also makes removing such statuses unnecessary—is made in Galatians, an attack on an embassy from Palestine that tried to convince uncircumcised followers of Jesus they needed to be circumcised. Paul points out that the embassy's insistence serves its own interest—a ploy familiar to Paul—and that Jesus' suspension of the Torah includes all its laws, with the exception of those connected with the scriptural covenant with Noah concerning not eating blood and not engaging in lewd practices like Noah's son Ham, which, as was apparently decided at a conference in Jerusalem between Paul and the heads of the assembly there, should apply to all humanity as offspring of Noah. All the rest of the Torah's laws depend on false distinctions among people. Circumcision was of such importance in Christian cells because in the Torah it is the first thing that separates sons of Abraham—Judeans, Arabs, and Idumeans like the Herods—from other people.

Paul's other letters include 1 Thessalonians, written to assuage anxieties about the impending cosmic war, and Romans, written to recommend the message that justification in Jesus the messiah makes justification by the laws of Judean torah, and hence the distinction between Judean and non-Judean, obsolete.

Sometime around the mid-50s, Paul decided to solidify support for his maverick leadership by pulling together a contribution of money from his cells in rich cities for the assembly in poor Jerusalem. He took the contribution to Jerusalem himself, where he was arrested, according to Luke, for conducting two non-Judeans into the temple in violation of an essential rule of temple purity. He claimed the right to be tried in a Roman court, and after trials before Roman officials in Caesarea ended up in Rome, in the reign of Nero. He is not heard of again until referred to in a letter from the end of the century, and may have been executed as a part of the attack on Christians after the great fire in Rome in 64.

The cells of the cult of Jesus were little persecuted, although its leaders could occasionally become mixed up in politics. James was put to death by the high priest Ananus in 62, who took advantage

of the temporary absence of the procurator and Agrippa's acqui-
escence to take the law into his own hands. Although the pharisees
may have played a role, the exact reason for the execution is not
known. Ananus, a descendant of the first high priest appointed by
Rome after the deposition of Archelaus in 6, later became the leader
of the revolt against Rome, in 66–67. James's place was taken by
Simon, another member of Jesus' family.

From the 40s on, rural unrest and guerrilla gangs, one numbered
by Josephus at thirty thousand men, plagued the Roman occupiers.
War did not break out until in 66 a collection of erstwhile high
priests, the wealthy oligarchs, broke with Roman authority at the
temple and rallied the Jerusalem mob, bandit gangs, and many
villagers to their side. Roman occupation, Roman incompetence,
Roman oppression, Judean religious sensitivity or zeal, class struggle, conflicts with gentiles in Palestine—all fueled the discontent the
leaders were able to exploit. But the deciding cause for the outbreak
was a shift in the strategy of the Judean elite created by the Romans:
instead of trying to rule the chaos on Rome's behalf, they used it
to build up factions reaching down through the social pyramid to
fight one another. Having lost the confidence of the procurators,
ambitious rulers turned to the gangs and the urban rabble for their
strength, appealing to them in the name of rebellion. The rebellious
leaders were also able to put the temple scriptures on their side.
From first to last the justification of the temple's jurisdiction, and
the primary impulse for conservatives' reform, had been in terms
of limiting state and debt slavery, even to the point of God's condemnation of the state, for those living at or below subsistence.
Relief from the exploitation of the labor of the poor was the constant
basis of the political nation's appeal for the support of the masses
already in Israelite and Judean history—the primary freedom that
liberation hermeneutics has refound in our time—and this is what
the Herodian elite now resorted to.

The immediate cause of the war was conflict over Judean rights
in Herod's gentile city Caesarea. An initial revolt was put down by
the procurator Florus, who continued to favor the gentiles in Caesarea, and at the same time raided the temple treasury. Subsequent
incidents showed that the rich were becoming more willing to win
favor with the urban mob by defiance, even on the pain of death,
than to keep the favor of the Romans. Temple officials then suspended sacrifices for the emperor. The Roman general in Antioch
marched south to quell the disturbance and met the resistance of

the Jerusalem crowds. At this point the frustrated Herodian elite seized the chance to foment a full-scale revolt. Jerusalem was taken by Judean forces, who restored the ruling high priest. The rebels turned Herod's temple and fortress into their main defense and started minting coins of a free Judean state already in May 66. One important gang gained early popularity by burning the debt archives (duplicates survived elsewhere). Though the fissures in Judean power soon became clear as factions fought each other as well as the Romans and those who sought accommodation with them, most Judeans supported the rebellion to the end, and not all under coercion.

The revolt pitted the rich against the rich. All the leaders promoted themselves as democrats but came from the ruling class, even Simon ben Gioras, the most important leader at the end of the war and the one usually thought most likely to be of lower class. The leader of the Zealots, a group formed in the winter of 68 as rural resistance groups moved into the capital before the advance of the Roman general Vespasian, was wealthy, although this small militant group, as outsiders, was hostile to urban rich, priests, and foreign rulers alike. Bands were held together by the traditional ties of family and patronage and recruited with promises of pay, booty, and power, more than of ideological or economic reform. None was based on sectarian identity.

The cult followers of Jesus of Nazareth looked for him in the turmoil, of precisely the kind expected to signal his return, but were disappointed. Otherwise they escaped involvement in the struggle against Rome, which was not their primary agenda. An uncertain tradition says the Jerusalem assembly migrated at the outbreak of hostilities to Pella, a Greek city in the Jordan Valley. In any case, thereafter they played little role in Palestine except in its Greek cities, where Jesus never went, especially Herod's Caesarea.

From the point of view of the capital, the Judean war was a foreign adventure of Nero, part of his Egyptian-based campaign against Ethiopia, designed to bolster his flagging authority at home. The strategy failed for Nero, but the war contributed greatly to his successor's legitimacy. Nero's General Vespasian, helped by his son Titus, a general among the forces in Egypt at the time, took Galilee, Perea, and parts of Judea in 68. After Nero died in 68, fighting stopped while Vespasian returned to Rome in 69 to compete for the emperorship, which he won after three others had seized and lost the job. Unduly prolonged by interruptions, the war was finished by Titus, who took Jerusalem in July 70 and destroyed the temple.

14

Old Scriptures, New Jurisdictions

With the temple went its ruling class. Unlike 587 B.C.E., in 70 C.E. the end was complete: no more temple, high priest, ruling priests, Sadducees, sacrifices, or Essenes, and no more kings. Some Judeans contrived to settle elsewhere under Rome's protection. Thousands died on the cross or were enslaved. Palestine fell under Roman military rule as a Roman province. Such complete destruction, which cleared the stage for the emergence of Judaism and Christianity, was not the usual Roman response to revolt. Rome preferred to go on dealing with a loyal remnant of the ruling class. But in this case Rome's creature, the Herodian priestly elite, had repaid Rome by rebelling. To such ingratitude there was only one response: utter spoliation.

Moreover, Palestine's fate hung once more on a succession crisis at the imperial court. With Nero's death in 68, Augustus's line came to an end. When General Vespasian of the Flavian family captured the emperorship in 69, the "year of four emperors," he determined to make his Judean war, now commanded by his son Titus, prove to his subjects and rivals that the gods were on his side and rebellion unwise. He had Titus devastate Judea and assume a near co-regency with him. He led Judean captives to their death or slavery in a triumphal parade in Rome. He built two triumphal arches depicting the war and the degradation of Judean prisoners (the Arch of Titus still stands today). He stamped coins with a portrait of Judea as a hostile adversary now crushed. He built a temple to Peace and deposited there the Judean temple's utensils, imitating Augustus, who had built a monument to victory over a foreign enemy to celebrate apparent Roman unity at the end of the civil war that brought him to power. He ordered the poll tax on Judeans that before had gone to the Judean temple paid to the temple of Jupiter in Rome. He shut down the harmless Judean temple at Leontopolis in Egypt. The Flavians founded their dynasty on Judean ruin: the greater the ruin, the greater their legitimacy.

The change of rule in Palestine wrought by Vespasian and Titus was chronicled in Greek in *The Judean War* by the pharisee Josephus, a rich Judean who deserted to the Romans early in the war, laid odds on Vespasian's triumph, and ended up a Flavian pensioner in Rome. There he joined Agrippa and his sister in Titus' circle and shared the last Herodian's memories of the nightmare of Judean rule. His account, deploring the rabble rousing and exonerating rich Judeans of complicity and Romans of excessive brutality in the conduct of the war, remains the primary source for this era.

With its elite dead or bedded in Rome, the Judean state and its jurisdiction disappeared beyond hope of restoration. Judeans and their practices continued to be tolerated only because they were numerous and, without temple and rulers, without direction. Judeans were a minority everywhere but Palestine, and in Palestine there were no major cities. Vespasian auctioned Judean land to non-Judeans and gave much of it to army veterans. During the war, some Judean deserters had been confined on an imperial estate in Jamnia on the coast, once Hasmonean land bequeathed by Salome to Augustus's wife Livia and by Livia to Tiberius. After the war, the heads of the pharisees were resettled there under a watchful Roman eye.

The temple and its inveterate, hobbled jurisdiction were gone, but the temple's scriptures, the written basis of its jurisdiction, survived everywhere there were Judeans, in the Persian and Roman empires alike. Stripped of temple and monarchy, Judeans faced fundamental questions: what jurisdiction would the scriptures now apply to, what would they mean in their new jurisdiction, and who would decide? The Torah, the main repository of law, finished between the destruction of the first temple and the building of the second, made no mention of the temple and therefore remained conveniently applicable to the new situation. Without the temple, however, the process by which its scriptures had been formed and applied, already dormant, ceased. No longer could new meanings be derived from and incorporated into the existing collection. The fire that burned the temple baked its scriptures, killing the yeast of their ongoing internal reinterpretation. The answers to the question of jurisdiction would now have to come from external interpretation.

The problem of Judean jurisdiction was a Roman one as well, and any Judean solution depended on the Roman solution. At first the Romans left the matter unsettled, making sure only that Judeans under urban jurisdictions kept the peace. Before it was settled, Rome was forced to put down a second struggle for an independent Judean state as furious as the first, the war of 132–135 led by Bar Kosiba (nicknamed Bar Kokhba, Star-man, from Num. 24:17). Thus the first Roman failure to achieve order was compounded by a second, which resulted in even harsher measures against Jerusalem and put the revival of Judean state-level jurisdiction with or without Roman support finally out of the question.

The pharisees and the bishops proved to be the Judean groups fittest to survive the new political situation, emerging over several centuries of adaptation to Roman rule, as the organizations of the Jewish pharisees (called rabbis, a title of honor given them by their students and clients) and the Christian bishops sanctioned by the empire. Building on existing solutions developed in the vacuum of authority under the Hasmoneans and Herodians, these two power sources provided two kinds of answers to the questions about the scriptures' future and thus gave us the Bible in its Jewish and Christian forms. The rabbis interpreted the scriptures in terms of *local* jurisdiction, the bishops in terms of *imperial* jurisdiction. These alternatives represented a forking or bifurcation of the scriptures' jurisdiction due to the loss of the middle, or state, level on which the temple had functioned. The split into two groups, Jews and Christians, with two sets of scriptures was reinforced by the policies of the two big powers, Rome and Persia, toward them during the next four centuries.

The cults, practices, and scriptures of both groups, rabbis and bishops, differed from those of the temple; thus we reserve the terms Jew, Jewish, and Judaism for the rabbis and those under their rule and use Judean, contrary to custom, for the common source of Judaism and Christianity, even though both sets of terms are the same in Hebrew and Greek. Despite the ostensible merging of Judean and Jew even in certain New Testament passages and by the rabbis who became rulers of Palestine in the third century and continued to use Hebrew and Aramaic more than Greek, the roots of Christianity were not Jewish. Christianity did not derive from the Judaism of the pharisees, but emerged like Judaism from the wider Judean milieu of the first century. Both Christians and Jews stemmed from pre-70 Judean-ism as heirs of groups that were to take on the role of primary guardians or interpreters of scripture as they developed on parallel tracks in relation to each other. Both were equally changed by the empire's destruction of the temple, defeat of Bar Kosiba's forces, and election of Christianity in the fourth century.

Local jurisdiction in Palestine after 70 devolved by default upon local landowners and leading village men and townsmen, wealthy elders, many not Judeans. Both Judeans and non-Judeans supported the synagogues in Palestine that were becoming centers for the local councils run by synagogue heads. These officials were in effect the magistrates, who until the beginning of the third century exercised the local jurisdiction among Judeans later assumed by the rabbis. The magistrates, secure in their growing wealth, cared little for the defunct law of the scriptures and the interpretations made popular by the pharisees.

Scriptures were left to the pharisees, settled as a community of saintly sages out of the way of the local magistracy and the Roman authorities. Their leader was Johanan ben Zakkai, who had escaped Jerusalem in a box during the height of the Roman siege and turned up on Vespasian's estate in Jamnia. Around him the pharisees organized the school and court that were the seed of Judaism. Under Johanan, they appointed themselves to the rights and duties of the sanhedrin, but had neither authority nor occasion to carry this presumption off. They abandoned the label pharisee, possibly due to Christian debasement of it into a synonym for hypocrite, in favor of the title rabbi.

As the remnant of the Judean intelligentsia in Palestine, the pharisees, or rabbis, continued their interpretation of law, stressing purity and prudence, and enjoyed support in town and village despite their lack of wealth to bolster their authority. They maintained their dialectic process of legal dispute; holders of the main opinions on a given issue were called *nasi*, "chief," and *ab*, "father." The theory of oral torah allowed them to accommodate and compromise and thus keep the scriptures workable.

Johanan's refusal to envision a restoration of the temple and his arrogation of temple authority made him unpopular. Gamaliel of the wealthy family of Hillel took his place, despite the family's participation in the revolt against the Romans. Gamaliel toured Judean communities in the empire sometime before 115, to preach and urge the authority of the rabbis to compatriots disoriented by the loss of the temple. Descendants of Hillel, who nursed the idea of a restored temple (with designs on its rule), dominated the pharisees into the third century and oversaw the codification of their oral law turned written in the Mishnah.

Rabbis, perhaps as early as their days at Jamnia, determined the canon of Hebrew scriptures we now have, deciding which scrolls from the temple collection were to be given the stamp of approval. The written Torah was the standard. Since in the rabbinic view it was produced by Ezra the scribe par excellence, nothing later than Ezra was admitted. The scriptures must be in Hebrew, or mostly so (Ezra itself was partly Aramaic). Exception was made for Daniel, written in 165, half in Aramaic, because it ostensibly took place during the Babylonian exile (thus it appears right after Ezekiel in the Christians' partly chronological canon), and because it took an accommodating apocalyptic stance against armed resistance. An opening section of Daniel and its last third fulfilled the Hebrew requirement. The rabbis' Bible went from Moses to Ezra, the concept of the Old Testament that prevails today in Jewish and Protestant circles. The Hasmonean scriptures were excluded because they did not accommodate imperial rule, and because the rabbis had bad memories of Alexander Janneus and good memories of Agrippa II and his Herodian predecessors.

The collection of 150 psalms was completed at this time, the last significant modification of a document in the Hebrew scriptures. Psalms 90–150 were organized, out of many psalms available for inclusion (the Christian canon ended up with 151 psalms; David was said to have written thousands). The whole was divided into five "books" like Moses' Torah by means of concluding doxologies. A psalm attributed to Moses was placed at the head of the part of the collection added to the Levitical psalter (Ps. 90), again to match the Torah. With the temple and its service gone, Psalms became the object of study and meditation, like the Torah, rather than a liturgical text. Its concluding orchestral bombast (Ps. 150) was balanced by a new opening psalm enjoining study of Torah, and by implication psalms, day and night as a source of wisdom (Ps. 1).

Five of the temple's later scrolls were grouped for reading during the five annual holidays whose rites compensated for the loss of the temple's rites: Song of Songs, a sumptuous dialogue of unrequited love, for Passover; Ruth, with its fruitful encounter during the wheat harvest, for Weeks; Lamentations, a complaint over the destruction of the temple, for the Tenth of Ab, the anniversary of the destruction; Ecclesiastes, advising "eat, drink, and be merry," for bacchanal Booths; and Esther for Purim. (No Hasmonean Hannukah.) These were placed before Ezra, Nehemiah, and Chronicles to preserve the Levitical framework of the Writings, which closed down prophecy.

The main organization competing with the rabbis for the privilege of deciding what the temple scriptures were now to mean was the collective churches of the Christian bishops in the cities of the Roman and, to a lesser extent, Persian empires. The Christian centers were the commercial and port cities of Caesarea (the Roman capital of Palestine), Antioch, Alexandria, Ephesus, Rome, and—after its founding in the fourth century as the new, Christian Rome—Constantinople. At the fall of the temple, the head assembly of Jesus' cult followers in Jerusalem lost its preeminence to the assemblies outside Palestine, especially Antioch, Alexandria, and Rome itself, where the loose organization of voluntary associations, headed by bishops supporting one another's authority, offered no more threat to Roman order than the rabbis' wide and weak authority. The messianism inherent in their name remained politically innocuous, making penultimate but not undermining Roman jurisdiction. Although in the world of Greco-Roman cults, Jesus was seen as a demigod, a son of God as described of royalty in the imperialist Psalm 2, the royalist implications of the title *christos* were ignored as harmless, as the authorities were more prepared than many Christians to see Jesus' return postponed. Local magistrates tended to take notice of the cult only when others took offense at their behavior, even with little justification.

Christians were less fitted than the pharisees to contribute to Judean governance, since they had developed no law for productive life, the application of torah as law having been suspended pending the return of Jesus "in power." Despite the tendency of the bishops, many Christians did maintain a Judean identity and adhere to the Torah's rules for purity in a Christian mold, but these lost influence in the course of the second century. After the second Judean war most Christians distanced themselves even further from the scorned name "Judean," and the rabbis began to tighten their hold on Palestine. In the emerging debate over how Palestine's purity was to be restored, the rigorous partisans of pharisaic piety made life difficult for the lax, including Christians, who from now on were little seen outside the cities in the land of their birth until led back by Constantine's mother. Even so, many Christians were still practicing circumcision and celebrating Passover at the end of the second century.

The Christian bishops promoted a new set of scriptures whose midrash, or interpretation, made their connection with the Hebrew scriptures explicit. The New Testament documents are nearly everywhere a commentary on or interpretation of the temple scriptures, even where not immediately obvious (citations in margins or footnotes in the New Testament typically indicate only a fraction of its pervasive references and allusions to the Old Testament). Not unlike Johanan ben Zakkai, the bishops favored writings showing that the temple service and its priesthood were not what the temple's Torah was really about. Once the temple no longer existed, Christians separated by mental and physical distance from its centrality could read its scriptures in a way that excluded the temple altogether, not just its particular purity regulations and taboos.

Although the collection was not called the New Testament before the third century (contemporary with the formation of the rabbis' Mishnah) and was not finally defined until the fourth century under imperial auspices, all the documents in it were written supposedly by apostles from the first generation or their immediate associates, just before and after the fall of the temple, and selected to explain what Jesus Christ meant for interpreting the scriptures in the light of Rome's temporary assumption of rule. The Christianity of the New Testament began not with the birth, death, or resurrection of Jesus, but with the end of the temple to which the first cell of his followers was attached. References to the first Judean war in the New Testament are rare and veiled, but the event is basic to the collection and many of its writings.

Taking God's anointed king Jesus, shamed in death and restored in resurrection, as the standard for making the temple scriptures still meaningful, the bishops' interpretation insisted on Roman law in the absence of temple law, until Jesus' return should inaugurate a new nontemple law. Over time, Jesus Christ represented the means to stand up under Roman jurisdiction, live with it, or exercise it, but in any case Roman jurisdiction was the given. Some Christians fell foul of Roman justice, but most took it for granted in practice if not in theory. Christian landowners ran their estates according to Roman law, all the while rabbinic jurists in Palestine were developing a new basis for Judean jurisdiction in estate management.

The empire's inclusive jurisdiction, crossing national, ethnic, and political boundaries, provided the matrix for the vast extension of Christian inclusiveness begun in the suspension of scriptural purity rules. Christians, whether Judean or not, inherited a legal identity that would keep them Judeans and give strict Judeans an advantage among them; and, in view of Roman peace and Jesus' imminent rule, they did not, at first, need to replace that legal identity with another. The struggle over whether Christian men had to be circumcized decided this issue, but not until long after Paul wrote Galatians. At a meeting held within twenty years of Jesus' death and described in a late first-century text (Acts 15), it was decided that the only law in Torah applicable to all followers was the taboo on eating blood, with corollaries, imposed on Noah and hence humanity without distinction. Aside from the conventional Stoic virtues, prescribed rules of behavior would be Rome's rather than the Torah's, except where Christian cells decided for themselves to do otherwise, often against the advice of what became the official Christian writings. For Christians the temple scriptures would provide not exclusionary rules, but evidence for the rule of Jesus, whose judgment, consistent with the scriptures, was universal, negating state and local jurisdictions. Jesus' rule was imperial in its own right and destined to override Roman jurisdiction as well, in time—which many followers were eager to shorten, again contrary to the writings selected by the bishops.

The New Testament falls into three parts, the Gospels, the letters of Paul, and other letters and documents, although early manuscripts did not promulgate the collection in just this form. The jurisdiction of Rome is the ground base of the Gospels, the history of a man's trial and execution by Rome, without resistance. Rome is in collusion with the temple and Judean leaders, on whom the Gospels, acquiescing in the Roman process, focus their censure and opposition. All four Gospels make the relation of Jesus to the destruction of the Judean temple of central significance, a theme required only after 70 and little considered by the temple-centered cells before, despite their anticipation of a cataclysmic war. Jesus scorned the temple, in its present form; his followers awaited its rectification, the object of God's transforming judgment, as foretold in the prophecies of God's war in Isaiah, Zephaniah, Zechariah, Joel, Daniel, and many other texts, and the seat of Jesus' judgment.

In the long view, writings about the saint Jesus clustered around the fall of the temple just as earlier the writings about the saints had clustered around the fall of Samaria and of the temple in Jerusalem. In the Christian Bible, the New Testament is a third collection of such fulfilled prophecies regarding the unjust state.

The Gospel of Mark set the genre of describing Jesus' deeds and words in terms of regarding the Judean war as God's war, in accord with scripture and Christian expectation, and the destruction of the temple as its outcome, ostensibly contrary to the scripture but not so to the enlightened Christian. On the basis of texts mainly from Exodus, Kings, Isaiah, and Malachi, Mark keyed Jesus to the end of the temple. Rival groups, especially the pharisees, it implicated with the temple and ridiculed by implying their fall in the wake of its destruction. Despite apparent earlier connections, the followers of Jesus had nothing to do with the likes of pharisees, whose oral law is void (" 'you nullify the word of God through your tradition' . . . he declared all foods clean"). Church heads like Peter, James (in name), and John, whose authority had depended on the temple, it discredited. Every hint of a national temple-centered implication of Jesus' movement and messianic title it made the subject of sharp irony. Jesus usurped Vespasian's royal status but laid aside, for the interim, its royal prerogatives. Thus the middle third of the Gospel, in which on the way to Jerusalem Jesus instructs his disciples that his is a submissive role, is framed with two healings of blind men, the first by a procedure nearly identical to that used by Vespasian in Alexandria on his way back to Judea after achieving the imperial crown. Roman taxes are to be paid, says the future king. Like all of Jesus' followers, the author of Mark expected Jesus to return in power soon. The Gospel was useful to church authorities whether he did or not.

As a timely interpretation of the temple scriptures in response to the loss of the temple, Mark became the norm for interpreting Jesus Christ and the scriptures for the new circumstances. Three of its revisions are represented by the other three Gospels. Insomuch as Mark initiated this interpretation, it marks the beginning of the New Testament as a collection and the Christian Old Testament as the collection's scriptural base.

Matthew enhanced the Gospel as a new torah by incorporating a previously composed string of Jesus' sayings (an anonymous "source," or *Quelle* in German, hence called "Q"), dividing Jesus' combined sayings into five groups, and placing the first group on a mountain analogous to Sinai. It enlarged on the struggle with the pharisees and their kind: Christians faced more trouble from synagogues and their puritans than from Rome, and had to distinguish their own brand of extremist behavior from that of fellow Judeans under Flavian censure. The rulings of Jesus in five parts served as the new torah of Jesus Christ, not the replacement of Moses but his fulfillment, in opposition not to the teachings of the pharisees but to their status-seeking practice of jurisdiction in the cities, their weak suit. Matthew's version of Mark was eventually positioned ahead of Mark because it laid down the jurisdiction of Peter, regarded by then to have been the first bishop of Rome. The Gospels were then arranged according to their likeness to Matthew: Mark, Luke, John.

Luke-Acts, a two-scroll work, begins at the temple, where Jesus keeps the torah scrupulously, and ends with Roman jurisdiction as Paul appeals to Caesar in Rome against false judgment by Judeans in Palestine. Jesus announces an era of debt remission and proceeds to apply it to everyone, forcing them to reassess their position. Luke-Acts parallels Jesus and Stephen, victims of Judean hostility, and Paul, but leaves the parallelism obviously incomplete by including a great deal about Judean hostility to Paul—the purported justification of his mission to non-Judeans—and nothing about the execution of Paul in Rome. This surprising omission was to avoid defaming the jurisdiction of Rome, which Paul so assiduously seeks, with responsibility for Paul's death, even when it must have been widely known. (At century's end, Paul's martyrdom was praised in a letter by the bishop of Rome.) In Luke-Acts the spirit of Jesus Christ comes into prominence, leading the church's crusade away from Levitical purity and toward inclusion on a Roman basis.

John features the *logos*, the word of creative judgment, or "case," which makes possible a radical distancing from social norms, as the heart of the conflict between Jesus and the "Judeans" (high priests and pharisees in the same camp), which prefigures the affliction of many Christians who were put out of synagogue assemblies during the 80s and 90s when Judeans had to decide their position on Judeans' legal rights. Under the circumstances, Christians must have seemed like chaff among the Judean wheat, disregarding the Torah, all that was left of Judean legal identity. John turns their stance inside out by putting in their mouths the climactic retort, "We have no king but Caesar," turning the implicit charge against the Christians back on the accusers. The theme remains legal justice, the vindication of Jesus and his followers against Judean hostility. Jesus serves as temple, law (*logos*), and everything else significant. Sometime after the writing of John, a second author added chapter 21, which affirms the primacy of Peter (and his successors in Rome). John's viewpoint and style appeared also in three letters eventually included in the New Testament.

Letters were still the prevalent form of writing in and among the far-flung churches of the empire, and they make up three-quarters of the New Testament documents. The bishops soon discovered the fresh usefulness of the rather difficult and idiosyncratic correspondence by that prewar pharisaic interpreter, the Roman citizen (a status still rare in the east) who spent much of his adult life, especially its finale, embroiled with empire courts. Paul's letters were mainly in defense of his commission to spread word about the justification, or new legal status, made possible by the elevated Jesus for Judeans and others in empire cities, far from the temple. For him, justification through Jesus already made the Torah's temple-based jurisdiction obsolete, though its rules might apply in the interim. Once a zealous opponent of Jesus' followers, Paul turned into an equally zealous convert, whose distinction was a categorical detachment from any practical jurisdiction other than that of the courts of Caesar. If he ever suffered in Palestine the lower prestige of an expatriate rabbi, Paul rose above it: justification by God was open to any and all "in Christ" and had nothing to do with the keeping of torah rulings, the sanctity of the temple or Palestine, or Judean integrity. Among the many learned emissaries for Judean parties in the empire, Paul stood out as an effective rhetorician, in writing at least, and he had put a fine point, repeatedly, on the legitimacy of his work in relation to the executives in Jerusalem and all other Judeans who adhered to Judean law.

For the churches' bishops Paul articulated the distinction between themselves and the Judeans of the empire who continued to call themselves, unfortunately, Judeans and to remain obedient to the Torah, whose rules without the temple were problematic. One letter, which laid out how non-Judeans and Judeans alike were to gain God's justification apart from the jurisdiction of the torah as usually understood, and which left the jurisdiction of Rome intact (Paul urged subordination, most accepted submission), was made a letter to Rome and placed at the head of a collection of Paul's letters circulated for the edification of the bishops' churches—or of those who could understand them. To this pharisee, the Torah remained "holy, just, and good," but no longer gave basis for facing God in judgment. Paul was primarily concerned with a person's right before God, or justification. His attempt to define rights outside the scope of law could lapse into abstraction, though for him the matter was never abstract and eventually cost him his life.

Ephesians was written in Paul's name to clarify the meaning of this collection. In effect it is the twenty-ninth chapter of Acts (which has only twenty-eight chapters), although in it the conflict depicted in Acts is transformed. The Paul of Ephesians writes while awaiting the trial in Rome that Acts leads up to. Paul imagines telling the emperor, when he sees him, that there is peace between Judean and non-Judean, meaning the supposed harmony they find "in Christ," not the real conflict that according to Acts landed Paul in jail and on trial. Paul says this peace he is going to recommend to Caesar on his day in court justifies his urging the churches to override the inherent social conflicts within them, between the more and less powerful—master and slave, husband and wife, parent and child—in order to represent peace to the powers that be. This fit the new church being run Roman-style by masters, husbands, and fathers, adapted to Roman administration of Roman peace.

Other documents furthering the congruence of house churches accepting slavery with the household of the Roman state with its slavery gradually gained authority with the churches' leaders. The pastoral letters made much of the office of bishop and urged prayer for the emperor. Hebrews dissolved the temple rites in a solution of Platonic speculation. Revelation scarcely made it into the collection, the veil of "Babylon," now Parthian, almost failing to conceal its condemnation of the Roman beast. The Shepherd of Hermas typifies writings that placed the laws of the "city of God" in clear opposition to the laws of the state; such works never made the canon.

As far as is known, nothing in the collection was written in final form in Palestine. It maintained the stances of inclusion, moderation, and deference to authority vital to the success of the bishops' organization in the imperial cities. The forms of midrash used by the Gospels, Paul, and the other New Testament writers are essentially the same as those used in the Talmuds, from the exegesis of individual verses of scripture to the interpretation of themes through independent narrative. In addition to Greek and glossolalia, Christians spoke various dialects of Hebrew, Aramaic, Egyptian, Phoenician, Punic, Latin, Armenian, Arabic, Persian, and later

Nubian, Ethiopic, Sogdian, Georgian, and Gothic as well, but the bishops' scriptures, as a collection meant to tie Christians as one, all spoke the empire's Greek. The hundreds of Christian writings that did not meet the churches' needs in theme or language were not to be found on the road to fourth-century canonization whose course was set during the first generation after the war that ended the temple. The New Testament had so little to do with the churches' own order that even the Didache, a primitive organizational manual, failed to find its place in it.

Due in part to the similar histories of the rabbinic and the episcopal organizations for their first two hundred years, the Christian New Testament shares features with its fellow heir to the Hebrew scriptures, the Mishnah, which was being compiled at the same time the New Testament was taking form as a collection. As the standard of scriptural interpretation in the New Testament Jesus Christ played a role comparable to that of the oral torah in the Mishnah. The New Testament had its own scheme of organization and was written in Greek by authors not mentioned in scripture, thus breaking the mold of the exclusive authority of the Hebrew scriptures in some of the same ways as the Mishnah did. However, the writers of the New Testament claim a special revelation and almost always base their points on exegesis of the Hebrew scriptures, and in this way are significantly different from the Mishnah.

Contrary to some of the developing New Testament's central themes, the loose organization behind its development was moving away from Jesus' and Paul's Cynic tendencies toward Stoic and Platonic authoritarianism, leaving irony and indirection to thrive in ecclesial backwaters. The liberation signaled by the churches' stunning doctrine of forgiveness, not least of debt, gradually slipped off the churches' agenda, until the empire's organization in the fourth century of great estates, including the churches', worked by serfs made the key freedom from debt a dead issue.

Meanwhile, in reaction to Flavian oppression, many of the senatorial elite and members of the royal household itself were attracted to Judean Cynical thought in both pharisaic and Christian forms, as preferable to the open hostility to rule of the likes of Demetrius the Cynic. Elite disaffection came to a head during the reign of Vespasian's second son, Domitian (81–96), who organized the only early official scapegoating of Christians (and similarly vulnerable groups) besides Nero's. In the last decades of the first century a Cynic alliance might have emerged, if the two main Judean groups had not been busy widening the gap between them instead of patching it up.

People in the empire became Christians and heard and read the Gospels and Christian letters with joy because they were alienated from their familial, social, economic, political, or cultural surroundings, from the world that enmeshed them—except when they were simply the poor clients of other Christians. But the church that received them had emerged from the destruction of its temple in such a way as to grow up, during centuries of rivalry with Judeans and Jews, into a new net, the church of imperial jurisdiction, able to build new temples no more just than the first all over the Roman Empire, able to solidify its identity in terms of theory confusing to people on the ground, able to oppress Jews in the west another sixteen hundred years. Endurance and martyrdom did not distinguish Christian from Jew, but the New Testament that nourished both Christian oppressed and Christian oppressor did.

The empire continued to expand during the reigns of Trajan (98–117) and Hadrian (117–138). At the end of Trajan's reign Judeans broke the peace in Libya, Egypt, and Cyprus, but apparently not Palestine. In 132 Hadrian banned circumcision everywhere, and the Judeans in Palestine led by Bar Kosiba launched the great second rebellion, two generations after the first, as though a second Babylonian exile were about to end. Many Judean wealthy supported the cause: there was little reason to defect into the hands of Roman officers who now had even less excuse for trusting Judeans. Rabbi Akiba at Jamnia gave his endorsement, but it is not likely, given their later survival, that all the rabbis went along. This second Judean war was every bit as brutal and disastrous as the first, but much less is known about it because of lack of sources. Bar Kosiba issued coins inscribed with the year of the "freedom of Israel," but the Romans won in 135. Hadrian razed a thousand villages, sold thousands of Judeans as slaves, cleared Jerusalem and its environs of all Judeans, renamed the city Aelia Capitolina and the land Syria Palestina. Towns and villages in Galilee grew for the next century, as Judeans abandoned the ravaged area to the south. The rabbis at Jamnia moved to Galilee.

15

Rabbis and Bishops
in the Empire

The catastrophic end of the second Judean war introduced a century of comparative political stability in Palestine and throughout the empire. From Antoninus Pius (138–161) through the last of the dynasty of Septimius Severus (193–235), the empire's borders were secure. Persia posed no threat: Severus established Roman provinces in western Mesopotamia, and the last of his dynasty sparred regularly with the new Sasanian rulers on their turf, not Rome's. Established cities prospered, as Antioch, Alexandria, Caesarea, and other eastern ports continued to supply Rome's bread, and new ones were built: for example, Severus founded Eleutheropolis not far from the site of Lachish, destined to become one of the great Byzantine cities of Palestine. The number of non-Italians in the Roman senate steadily grew, and all freemen became citizens in 212. Sheltered by more Roman peace, rabbis and bishops went about enhancing their power with little hindrance and occasional aid from the empire.

The ruling cult of the empire's cities was dedicated to the empire and eventually to the emperor himself. Responsible officials maintained its observances: sacrifices by magistrates, auspices taken on occasions of state, senate sessions in sacred precincts, construction and care of temples and statues, deposit of war spoils in temples, state-sponsored festivals and games, regular election of a host of minor officials of state, and other forms of compliance with sacral law. It required little, however, of the empire's subjects, beyond occasional acknowledgment. In contrast to the imperial cult's white noise, the drone of Judean and Christian callings required choice, dedication, and intolerance of other commitment.

After the tumult of the first and second centuries, a minority of Judeans was left in Palestine. Galilee, on the periphery of Bar Kosiba's war of liberation, became the center of Judean life for those who had not emigrated to the cities of the empire and of Persian Babylonia and elsewhere but no longer ranked among the first Judean communities in wealth and size. Most of the rabbis of Jamnia, distancing themselves from Akiba's support of the revolt, chose to relocate to Usha in lowland Galilee, near the coast, where they could maneuver for control of the land whose purity they cherished.

As artisan scholars with few local ties, the rabbis were slow to establish their authority among the landowning magistracy, who sponsored the local synagogues proliferating in shops, homes, and soon special buildings. They associated with local landowners, who shunned their extremist piety, only through taking their sons as students in their peculiar non-Greek, non-Platonic, non-philosophical schools. While magistrates continued to hear most civil and criminal cases, the rabbis' jurisdiction, grounded in the pharisees' principle that priestly cleanness could be achieved in homes out in the land as well as in the temple, covered the purity of food, clothing, pots, furniture, menstrual women, and corpses, tithes in their support, Sabbath work rules, small parts of synagogue ritual (mostly in the hands of the magistrates), vows, and fasts. Their most important prerogative was to set the ritual calendar, particularly the Day of Atonement, their foot in the door to greater authority. Though not comprehensive, their rulings covered a range of local, daily, essential activities, which allowed them scope to assume advising magistrates and eventually, by the fourth century, to extend their moral and religious authority to handle cases themselves.

The rabbis' authority expanded under Rabbi Judah (170–220) of the house of Hillel, the first to monopolize the title of *nasi* and to hand leadership to his less qualified sons as a dynastic inheritance. Under his control the rabbinic academy moved to Beth Shearim and then to the Greek town of Sepphoris (where it interacted with a persistent cell of Christians). Judah was a powerful landowner and exporter in his own right, a rabbinic aristocrat who owned olive groves and vineyards in many parts of Palestine, great tracts of fertile arable in the Jezreel Valley and in the Golan, balsam groves in the Jordan Valley, rich sources of linen and wool, and an extensive fishing fleet. His wealth and noble bearing—he insisted on formal greetings from his students and clients, including the thousands of workers on his estates—were bound to earn the Romans' respect. Rome supplied his successors with palace guards, including Gothic and German bodyguards, to protect their client. Fellow landowners were gratified by Judah's rabbinic rulings which took cognizance of their needs. Judah's welcome in the imperial court was enhanced by the growth of the rabbis' authority in Galilee (resistance to this development from Babylon did not bother the Romans) and by the growing prestige and power of intellectuals like the sophists in the empire's ruling circles.

This rabbinic prince oversaw the codification of two centuries of rabbinic rulings in the Mishnah, the first recording of such rulings in writing, contrary to centuries of practice, and the first time they had been backed by force. In answer to the question what, given the loss of the temple, remained of its sanctity and the sanctity of its priests, land, and people, the Mishnah declared they continued to be sanctified through the keeping of Moses' oral torah, the standard for external interpretation of the scriptures. While the contemporary New Testament stressed the scriptures' prophetic character and left rules about life to relative generalities and radical dictums like the requirement of forgiveness, the Mishnah, though in some sense an extension of P, made little direct reference to the scriptures and so before long required further midrash supplementation.

The Mishnah's sixty-two tractates in six divisions cover land and its use, sacred times, family relationships, civil damages and court procedures, the temple and its cult (in case of restoration), and purity of food preparation and consumption. Four of the six divisions take the temple as the source of holiness and avoidance of uncleanness defined in Levitical terms. Thus the ideal of the temple was reintegrated into the regulation of prayer and daily activity in order to resanctify Judean lives in home, village, and town, and so revive the ideal of a sanctified nation obedient to God. Pharisaic interest in the temple per se probably grew to this extent only after the priesthood itself was defunct. The centrality of the temple in the Mishnah makes it in part what Neusner calls "an act of imagination in defiance of reality" and hence a statement of faith as well as of purity and right, which left much open to current judgment.

The rabbis' rulings on issues in common life, which often seem trivial to Christians influenced by polemic like Matthew's, attempted to balance the vital interests of rich and poor. A person surviving on gleanings, for example, would not consider the pronouncements of the tractate on what constitutes gleanings of the poor as nit-picking, nor would the landowner and the gang boss. Many of the rabbis' rulings on debt were designed to reach practical agreement with Judean landowners, who were thus encouraged to allow the rabbis to handle more cases. Thus the tractate dealing with the debt remission in the seventh year laid down in Deuteronomy 15:1 pertains more to the land's rest than to the workers' rest or debt relief, as in P. Debt remission is a rare topic in the Mishnah. The needs of the poor, however, were not ignored. One ruling determined that "a loan secured by prozbul is not cancelled in the seventh year" (Sheb. 10:3). A prozbul was a contract taken out in court by a creditor that permitted him to collect on the debt at any time. "When Hillel," this ruling explained, "saw that people refrained from giving loans to one another, transgressing what is written in the Torah, he instituted this law"—also contrary to the Torah. Hillel believed it was better for the poor to receive a noncancellable loan than none at all, and decided prozbul (in existence all along in one form or another) was the best means to this end. This solution is typical of the compromises finally recorded in writing.

The pronouncements of the rabbis were regarded as an oral Torah parallel to the written Torah of the scriptures and of equal authority. The Mishnah makes occasional reference to the scriptures, but does not rely on them in any way to justify the authority of the sages, which is assumed without discussion: its authors are not authorities named in the scriptures; they used a contemporary Hebrew quite unlike the biblical idiom; they made no explicit declaration regarding special revelation (no quotations from God, unlike the scriptures); and they justified their pronouncements by the exegesis of scripture only rarely. Even when they cited scripture, they tended to do so in their own words. In the light of the Mishnah, the written Torah of the scriptures was seen to be only one part of the complete dual Torah.

At the same time it made no defense of its authority, the Mishnah made few absolute rulings. Consistent with the dialectic approach of the pharisees, in which the process of seeking meaning is all, nearly every case raised in the Mishnah is addressed by contradictory rulings presented in the form of disputes over common points. Nevertheless, under Roman auspices this codification of rulings became the basis of local Judean jurisdiction in place of state government—or at least of the authority of the rule makers.

The Bar Kosiba war was a watershed in Christian-Judean relations. In the beginning of the second century, the leader of the Christian cell in Ephesus wore the insignia of a Judean high priest and assumed he was leader of local Judeans as well; the eight bishops who succeeded him all belonged to his family, treating the office as a quasi-priestly inheritance. Likewise in Asia, later in the second century Melito of Sardis wrote a homily on the passion of Jesus in the style of a Judean Passover haggadah (ritual narrative). In the aftermath of the revolt, most Christians, still for some time to come a minority among Judeans, strove to distance themselves from their Judean roots, to avoid being tainted by association with what were seen as misguided, defeated, and discredited aspirations.

Thereafter, even though the emperor still regarded Christians and Judeans as related if not the same, drawing the distinction between the two seemed more essential than ever. Practices tied to the Judean past were increasingly neglected or rejected. Letters and documents opposing such practices, like the letters of Ignatius, bishop of Antioch, found vindication and popularity. A pseudepigraph of Barnabas succeeded in removing the Judean aspects of the Torah through allegorizing. In the third century, when both bishops and rabbis debated similar issues, such as whether idolatry, apostasy, or bloodshed could be forgiven, the church distanced itself from the Jewish positions. As the church hierarchy became increasingly Greek, Christians became the focal point of the old hostility between Greeks and Judeans in the cities.

Many Christians were inclined to throw the temple scriptures out along with other trappings of their Judean heritage, granting Judean claims to be the true heirs of temple institutions and wanting nothing to do with them. In the end, the Judean practices were eliminated, while the Christians' Judean scriptures were retained. The scriptures survived once again on their gift for legitimating authority in contests for power. In this case, the churches' bishops turned to scripture to sanction their authority against challenges from Marcionism, Gnosticism, and Montanism.

Marcion, a rich shipper from Pontus who preached in the churches of Asia, drew from Paul that torah and gospel have nothing to do with each other, nor the scriptural God with the God of Jesus Christ, nor the churches' authority based on the scriptures with the freedom of Christians in Christ. To support his point, he discarded most of the future New Testament, produced versions of Paul's letters and Luke purified of supposed Judean insertions, and rested his case on these. With this message he went to the churches' center in Rome, became a major donor there, and found many followers. Thrown out of Rome, he attracted a large following for his popular views and founded cells in many parts of Asia. He also headed his own organization of bishops, an urgent challenge to the non-Marcionite bishops. Marcion's churches spread all over the Mediterranean and lasted for several centuries.

Most bishops regarded Marcionism as a species of Gnosticism, a catchall term for a variety of pseudo-Platonic views and practices based on the idea that the only world that matters is the "logical" world—rational or irrational, but hinging on a word or Word (Greek: *logos*)—hiding beyond the world of the senses. The individual's spirit lies trapped in the present world, but can escape to the real world by true knowledge (Greek: *gnosis*), for Christians represented as word and wisdom in the person of Christ. Such knowledge was available to anyone and did not require a bishop to dispense it.

The bishops' response came in the arguments of Diognetus, Justin, Irenaeus, and Clement. Diognetus showed that Christian faith was rooted in the temple scriptures interpreted as prophecy rather than law. The right understanding of Christian prophecy depended on the right interpretation of the scriptures and not on direct access. For Justin, the churches that retained the temple scriptures were the true successors of the people of God described in them. Justin was a Greek from Samaria who put himself through a rigorous philosophical training and ended up a Christian in Rome, where he made philosophical treatment of the faith respectable by making explicit its Platonist and Stoic implications.

Irenaeus, bishop of Lyons (177–202) in Gaul, defended the unity of the Christian scriptures, old and new, and through them the unity of the church under the bishops. He argued against Marcion's selective use of the Gospels; to him the Marcionites had a reduced, "circumcised" gospel in place of an inviolable whole. He emphasized the apostolic tradition as the foundation of the bishops' authority and the authority of Christian writings the bishops defined as apostolic. Against the Gnostics' spiritual license he balanced the weight of material creation, exemplified in the bond between the temple scriptures and their fulfillment in the churches, in the incarnation of Christ as real humanity, and in Christ's embodiment in the episcopate. Against the Gnostics' unrestrained claim to authority he advanced the authority of the scriptures, whose interpretation the bishops as the churches' heads controlled. Grateful for his support of their class interests, the bishops tried to make Irenaeus as popular as the Gnostics, and early papyri of Irenaeus have shown up as far from Lyons as Egypt, a Gnostic home ground.

Clement, a contemporary of Irenaeus who taught in Alexandria, refined the merging of Christian and Platonist thought. He used Plato as well as Genesis to demonstrate that since God created this world it is not evil, but the only arena where God works to save people, in particular through the incarnation. The way to salvation begins with faith and lies through practice of the Stoic virtues of prudence, moderation, and patience. The pinnacle of Platonist interpretation was reached by Clement's student Origen, who taught in Alexandria and Caesarea until being tortured to death in Decius's persecution in 253. Origen rescued Platonist thought from hostile Platonists to use for Christian purposes. He combined great textual learning with brilliant imagination and piety, and while not everyone agreed with his thought, especially in the rival schools of Antioch, his influence on the developing episcopate was great. Origen's concept of salvation focused on the Platonist individual and did not extend to reforming society. One of his disciples became famous by specializing in exorcisms among the peasants of Pontus. Another became bishop of Alexandria and was outraged by Christians who advocated revolution; he wrote a critique of Revelation's grammar and style to show that since it could not have been written by John and therefore lacked apostolic authority, there would be no revolution. Another taught Eusebius of Caesarea, Constantine's court apologist.

Not all challenges to episcopal authority could be unanimously condemned by the bishops. Montanists, the followers of the self-proclaimed prophet Montanus of Phrygia, opposed practices that tended to merge Christian life with the Greco-Roman life of the empire, and claimed, like numerous Christians before them, the authority of the Spirit to rebel against bishops and deacons who resisted their views. Montanism arose in 156 in reaction to the execution of the most famous Christian leader in Asia, Polycarp of Smyrna, whose letters quickly became popular. Many were attracted to their piety, especially in reaction to the corruption of the wealthy church establishment, and their numerous churches lasted into the fifth century. Even Irenaeus sided with bishops who were inclined not to ban them.

The intellectual justification of episcopal authority put the bishops in debt to both Platonist philosophy and the Judean scriptures. From then on the alliance between urban Christian faith and practice on the one hand and a philosophy based on an ideal, invisible, and hierarchical unity (like God) manifested in material (Christ, churches, and bishops) fostered in intellectual centers like Alexandria and Rome was complete and indispensable. Non-Christian Neoplatonists were put out enough to lobby against this alliance, sometimes with fatal consequences for Christians. Sophistic and Cynic resistance to idealism went underground in the churches, until the spread of the monastic movement in the fourth century.

From then on the Old Testament remained a part of the Christian scriptures, at least in theory. The Old Testament, as it was called by Clement on the basis of a phrase in Paul's letters, was regarded as prophecy, pointing to the new law of God over against the old law of Moses and the Levites. Through the unity of the scriptures maintained by the episcopate, it was the source of the intolerant monotheism that distinguished the authoritative, exclusive, strict cult of Jesus Christ from the urban cults of the empire and eventually enabled it to replace them. The legal function of scripture, defining jurisdiction over the lives of Christians, remained in the hands of the bishops, who continued to leave the practical details to Stoic morals and imperial law.

In the Christian Old Testament, Hasmonean and Greek documents rejected by the rabbis retained their authority, as well as longer Greek versions of Esther, Daniel, and Psalms. In some cases, as with Samuel and Jeremiah, Christians preserved the Greek translations of Hebrew texts that were better than those of the rabbis. The documents were arranged by a combination of genre and chronology. The history in the Torah and Former Prophets was continued through Chronicles, Ezra, Nehemiah, and Esther. Then the great poetic works of David and Solomon were entered. Prophecy brought up the end, looking forward to its fulfillment. The scriptures were translated into many vernaculars, including Latin (especially in Africa), which after the fourth century became increasingly popular in the west.

Christian cells grew in numbers and muted fame. Publicists and polemicists, merchants and travelers visited Judean settlements and colonies and their synagogues and reported their debates among non-Judeans. Christian schools attracted followers. Impressed by miraculous works and even martyrdom, people were won to belief or trust (*pistis*) in the power (*dynamis*, also translated "miracle") of the Christians' patron deity to be effective, accomplish set goals, and bestow benefits. Converts usually remained ignorant of doctrine and rarely attended church. What they looked for was foreknowledge, safety, prosperity, good crops, and (especially from Christian cult) good health.

The church, as an increasingly wealthy mutual aid society, did have the power to bestow benefits. Its endowment in lands and wealth, constantly augmented, distinguished the cult of Jesus from the cults of other eastern gods and demigods. Bishops posed as minor urban princes. Origen complained about preachers catering to their congregations, bishops (especially in large cities) who imitated government officials and terrorized the poor, and deacons dipping into church funds for their private use. For centuries churches themselves could not own property. The churches' wealth—land, cell houses, cemeteries, property, money—was held by the bishops and designated deacons, who found it difficult not to confuse church property with their own. Not until the Rescript of Gallienus in 261 did empire law implicitly acknowledge bishops' legal status as officers of Christian assemblies, and not until Constantine could churches as companies hold property.

Besides material benefits, for many Christians faith meant that subordination or submission to Rome's jurisdiction in lieu of their own manifested God's ultimate jurisdiction over Rome as well as themselves. This was their understanding of Christ's death, and of Paul's plea not to take cases between Christians to civil court. This reading of the faith and scriptures can be grasped by setting the earliest creed, or rule of faith, recited as part of the initiatory rite of immersion, in which the noviate was thought to go through death to life, and accepted by Irenaeus as a norm for scriptural authority (hence Apostles' Creed), in the context of alienation from the world's jurisdiction as expressed in Mark and Paul.

"I trust in God," like Mark's "Trust in God . . . and say to this temple mount 'Be cast into the sea,'" referred to the trust that temple jurisdictions will be replaced by God's favorable judgment of those who forgive each other and thus make the temple as regulator of right and wrong superfluous. "I trust in Jesus Christ who shall come to judge the living and dead": Christ as God's monarch exercises God's jurisdiction. "I trust in the Holy Spirit": "Whoever blasphemes against the Holy Spirit never has forgiveness," because "they will deliver you up to councils, and you will be beaten in synagogues, and you will stand before governors and kings for my sake, to bear witness before them [to God's jurisdiction]. When they bring you to trial, do not worry ahead of time what you are going to say; say whatever you have to at the time, for it is not you who speak but the Holy Spirit." Since the Spirit speaks for you at the decisive trial, you are not to berate it. "I trust the church" whose jurisdiction derives from Christ and Peter and those like him and no other; "the communion of saints," who will, as Paul said, judge the world; "forgiveness of sins," which makes all jurisdictions superfluous; "the resurrection of the body," which makes the empire's judgment inconsequential; and "eternal life," the ultimate boon of God's rule.

This trust led many Christians to mortal witness. The seditious title *christos*, with its royalist implications, had the potential of creating serious social disturbance, although among the powerful it was subject more to philosophical than political debate. In line with the bishops' emphasis on scripture as prophecy, in practice Christ was taken as a prophetic rather than royal title, and most Christians looked to the future rather than the present for vindication. Roman authority, however, could regard it as a threat and punish those who proclaimed it, though the usual Roman response was to regard it as harmless belief. Most bishops did not condone taking Christ as an anti-Roman title, but emphasized Christ as *logos*, the basis of the word and witness of the martyred examples of faith, whom they honored greatly.

The century of stability that ended with the collapse of the Severan dynasty in 235 was followed by a century of political and economic upheaval, as one military strongman after another competed for the throne. Thirty emperors ruled in the first fifty years of the century, of whom one escaped murder. Central authority weakened. Army units backed their own generals all over the empire, but especially along the two great military frontiers, the long German frontier and the eastern frontier with Persia. Meanwhile the vigorous new dynasty in Persia, the Sasanians, picked off border cities and lands at Rome's expense. Increased military expenditure combined with a reduced tax base and loss of trade income to produce inflation; taxes were then levied in kind rather than worthless money. The urban rich who survived the chaos shifted their investments further into land and escaped the pressure to make up deficits and finance urban services and cults by moving to large estates.

The revival of Persian power brought Rome to the verge of dividing its empire into eastern and western spheres. When the Sasanians captured the emperor Valerian in 260 and sacked Antioch, Odenathus, the prince of Palmyra, a desert trading city on the Roman-Persian border, did Rome the favor of recapturing this territory and Antioch, and even attacked the Persian capital of Ctesiphon in Babylonia. In return Rome was obliged to make him the emperor's deputy to rule the "whole east." Odenathus's ambitions, halted by his death in 267, passed with his rule to his formidable wife, Zenobia. With the aid of a great Arab alliance (the Arabs later called Zenobia a dragon lady), Emperor Aurelian's Roman forces retook the east. Zenobia retired to Rome and married a senator.

Aurelian (270–275) tried to reunite the fragmented empire by bolstering imperial ceremonial (he required court visitors to kiss his big toe instead of his cheek) and by promoting a new cult of the unconquered sun (*sol invictus*), an offshoot of the military cult of Mithraism. Aurelian remilitarized the empire's borders under his direct rule and fortified many of its great cities, including its suburbs in an expanded wall around Rome.

Diocletian (284–305), intensifying the buildup and deployment of military defenses under central control, divided the empire into four sections and took charge himself in the east. A native of the Balkans like many of the military men on the imperial throne, he avoided Rome. He created a chain of border fortresses in eastern Palestine, again with help of Arab allies, which made Palestine again a focus of imperial interest. Diocletian's reign marked the official change of the emperor's mandate from that of *princeps* (first citizen) to *dominus* (master, military dictator). In his view, imperial authority had to be free of all legal limitation in order to inhibit the erosion it had suffered since the Severans. From Diocletian on the emperors were complete autocrats.

Diocletian's efforts to stem decay, confirmed by his successor Constantine, produced nearly three hundred years of political stability in the east. His "reforms" favored wealthy landholders and encouraged the growth of large estates worked by serfs and slaves, while they increased control over poorer people's livelihood through requiring occupations to become hereditary corporations, or guilds, expanding enforced public services, and levying heavier taxes (the opposite of Josiah's "reform" strategy). As currency proved hopelessly unstable, Diocletian resorted to payment in kind for the imperial income and offered incentives for maximum agricultural output. Christian bishops, as absentee though not hereditary estate holders, benefited from these opportunities to expand their power in the fourth century.

The insecurity along Rome's borders brought Palestine yet another shift of land ownership into large estates. Small Judean landholders lost their property to wealthy ones, often non-Judeans; tenant farming and day labor increased; much of the land, for the first time in such upheaval, was left to waste. As large estate holders exempt from Roman taxes, the leading rabbis were able to consolidate their power. Their rulings continued to accommodate the interests of fellow landowners, while conciliating their humble clients. For example, the ruling on the limitation of squatters' rights effectively gave greater rights to absentee landowners: properties could be worked by tenants and managed by factors. The estate owners, often callous patrons, made their fortunes foreclosing on debt, but shielded their own clients from rival tax farmers. When their bloated power came in jeopardy of collapse in the fourth century, rabbis consoled their clients, who might likewise be imagined to suffer, with the assurance that God looked after the welfare of the wealthy baron as much as the poor peasant.

With Roman authority too distraught to attend to them, the rabbis' influence as landholders and as possessors of the only codified law in Palestine continued to grow. By now they had located their school in Tiberias, which remained the main Jewish center in Palestine for many centuries. Here the Masoretic (vocalized) text of the Hebrew scriptures, which became the accepted version, was established during the sixth to ninth centuries. Thirteen synagogues, including one for Babylonian Judeans and one for Antiochan Judeans, were built. The most famous rabbi of the later third century, Judah Nesiah, grandson of the *nasi* Rabbi Judah (by this time *nasi* designated the head of the Jewish community), presided over a working sanhedrin, controlling administration in Palestine, regularly sending apostles to far-flung Jewish communities, collecting funds, appointing judges, and ordaining rabbis. Judah Nesiah wore royal clothing and had his own police force of armed slaves. Some time during this period or in the fourth century (precisely when is uncertain), the *nasi* was made ethnarch of the empire's Judeans, completing their merger with the rabbis' Jews.

Rabbinic influence reached to Babylonia also, where Judeans had been settled since the Persian period and were several times more numerous than in Palestine. Rabbi Judah taught Abba Arika, known as Rab, who founded a school in Babylonia at Sura, under Persian rule. The Mishnah was thus conveyed to Babylon soon after its composition. Rab's contemporary Samuel headed the school at Ne-hardea. His most famous saying encapsulated the necessity of com-promise with imperial power in terms the same as, in theory, the Christian view: "The law of the state is law." However, Judeans under Persian rule, like those under Roman rule, conducted their own courts where, as in Palestine, the rabbis gradually gained sway.

The rabbis' uniquely adaptable codification of local law, the Mish-nah, became increasingly authoritative in the wake of their rise to power. The dialectic process that produced it allowed for continuous change and supplementation. About 250, in the tractate Pirke Aboth (Sayings of the Fathers) added to the Mishnah, the first attempt was made to draw a clear theoretical connection between the Mish-nah and the Hebrew scriptures. According to this new tractate, "Moses received the [oral] torah and handed it on" through a series of sages to five pairs of named sages ending with Hillel and Sham-mai, themselves mentioned hundreds of times in the Mishnah, and down to the Mishnah's present. The chain of transmission of wise sayings, almost all recommending prudence in one form or another, therefore ran unbroken from Moses to the Palestinian rabbis. This theory grounded the Mishnah's autonomy in an explicit source of authority.

In an increasingly militarized society, the cult of Mithra spread along with other exotic eastern cults, first through the army, then more widely. As it fostered acceptance of the existing social order, Mithraism attracted people under orders, like soldiers and slaves. Its men-only feasting societies celebrating bull sacrifice multiplied along the military borders but had limited popularity in cities and among the populace as a whole. Aurelian's *sol invictus* was known among Mithra's devotees to be an epithet of their god but not promulgated as such. By contrast the Christian cult, with its base in great commercial population centers, large endowment in prop-erty, and inclusion of women and families as well as military men, was to prove the more lasting bulwark for empire.

Before their eventual triumph, however, Christians in the post-Severan era suffered three brief but intense bouts of imperial per-secution that loomed large in the writings and politics of the church. For a time the writings of the martyr Cyprian were more popular in the churches than Paul's, and probably the other New Testament writings as well. The death of Emperor Decius (249–50), and the

Persians' capture of Valerian (257–59) seemed to prove that their persecution policies were losers. Nevertheless in the face of the aggrandizing churches, Diocletian issued four edicts of persecution between 303 and 305 and the policy continued in force until 311. The first edict's requirement that litigants sacrifice to the emperor if they wanted to bring a case before an imperial court removed Christians' basic legal rights. Persecution on a grand scale was now established as a tool of imperial policy that could henceforth be turned for or against any cult. Before long Christians were the beneficiaries, and then only certain Christians, as imperial persecution of Christians turned into Christian persecution of Christians in the fourth and fifth centuries.

Hardship was not only imposed, but also voluntarily assumed by Christians, as many chose the living martyrdom of monastic asceticism. Monks, originally "loners" (Greek *monos*, alone) displaced in the post-Severan upheavals, fled the troubled world and gathered in saintly communities. The movement began under the leadership of the hermit Antony in the late third century in Egypt among the thousands of laborers thrown off their land. Although they shunned urban life and learning, some of these groups kept Gnosticism alive, as shown by the Nag Hammadi documents discovered in middle Egypt, from a fourth- and fifth-century community founded by the monastic leader Pachomius. Bound to survive in some form, the monastic movement became an institution in the fourth century with the establishment of Christianity as the imperial cult. Monastic estates, which shared the churches' tax-free status, offered workers the attraction of farming collectively without landlords' interference and keeping most of their product. These communities produced many of the most famous saints of the end of the biblical period.

Along with the monks' asceticism, an incipient split between the adherents of Platonism in Alexandria and the more down-to-earth philosophers in Antioch that was to figure in the imperial churches' theological and political debates emerged in this period. Paul of Samosata, bishop of Antioch, claimed that Jesus was a man who became divine rather than God who became a man. Through his pupil Lucian of Antioch, his teaching became the foundation of the Arian movement of the fourth century, the leading counter to episcopal authority. Paul was deposed by a synod of bishops in 268, but was saved from loss of his properties by his patron Zenobia, then ruling Antioch. Once Aurelian regained Antioch, the bishops prevailed on him to dispossess Bishop Paul—a foretaste of future military interference by the emperor in the affairs of the church.

When Diocletian retired in 305 to his palatial villa on the Adriatic coast, a civil war broke out that dwarfed the year of the emperors in 69. For nineteen years, 305–24, six claimants battled over the throne. Constantine, another Balkan general and son of the military governor of Rome's northwest territories, was proclaimed emperor in the west, co-regent with Licinius, in 306. In 312, at Mulvian Bridge, he conquered Italy under what he saw as the sign of the cross of Christ flaming in the sky with the command "in this [sign] conquer." No better proof was needed for the military dictator to adopt Christianity as his cult. Constantine's Edict of Milan in 313, declaring toleration for all cults, allowed him to establish Christianity as the imperial cult and ensured the Bible's role in Western history.

16

Constantine's Christian Triumph

Along with the fall of the temple, the most important event in the formation of the Jewish and Christian organizations and their scriptures was the establishment of Christianity as the favored cult of the Roman Empire at the beginning of the fourth century. In a dramatic reversal of official policy, the churches, for 250 years the object of mere tolerance and occasionally of vicious scapegoating and persecution, replaced the Roman state cults as the favored, then official, religion of the empire, the cultic mortar of the state. The converse of the establishment of Christianity was the disestablishment of the Jewish patriarchate. In both cases, the effect on the Bible was great.

Constantine, an army bastard, seized and held power by military might and murder: he had his co-regent Licinius and Licinius's son executed, also his own son and then, in remorse, the wife who had brought charges against their son. Once on the throne the new ruler inaugurated his regime by the time-honored device of establishing a new cult in a new city. In his lifelong search for legitimacy, the cult of his mother, a Christian like many women of aristocratic families, played a key role, though he himself, knowing what acts a ruler must commit, was not baptized until just before his death. To justify his seizure of power, Constantine needed a cult that was royal, universal, inclusive, peaceable, submissive, wealthy, numerous, eastern, and infiltrated in Persia. The cult of Jesus Christ served.

Besides guaranteeing Constantine's military victory at Mulvian Bridge, Christianity offered the emperor a way to redefine the basis of his autocratic powers. The Edict of Milan cleared the way for the emperor's patronage of the church by prescribing toleration for all cults, including Christianity. It recognized the churches as a corporate body and required the restoration to the bishops of properties confiscated during the persecution of Diocletian. The edict was a power play that freed Constantine from obligations to the traditional cults of the empire, like those of Mithra and of the Egyptian gods Isis and Serapis, and their aristocratic and military patrons, as well as the old Roman elite. Constantine's soldiers, even non-Christians, were taught to pray: "We acknowledge you [the Christian god] as the only God, we recognize you as king, we invoke you as ally, by you we have gained victories, through you we are superior to our enemies, to you we declare thanks for past benefits and we hope for future favors; we are your suppliants, imploring you to preserve to us for the longest time of life, safe and victorious, our emperor Constantine and his God-beloved sons."

In 324 Constantine defeated Licinius and began his rule of the entire empire, west and east. He moved the imperial capital east to the town of Byzantium on the Bosporus, which he enlarged and renamed Constantinople, the "City of Constantine," just as David had named Jerusalem the "City of David." Legend said that Constantine was shown the site by an angel, who led the emperor and his court on a hike around a territory three times larger than the existing town. The corvée gangs were put to work, and enough of the new city was completed for it to be dedicated by Christian bishops in honor of the Virgin Mary as the official imperial residence in 330. People flocked to the new capital, which quickly outgrew its sacred bounds, on the way to becoming the largest city in the western world for over a thousand years. The new capital became the center of the vast powerful bureaucracy, often staffed with Christian clerics, that taxed and governed the empire. It lay within closer reach of shipments of taxes in kind, especially from the rich eastern grain lands in Egypt and Syria, and less within reach of Rome's old aristocracy. It also placed the imperial armed forces closer to the two main military fronts, one against the Germans on the Danube and the other against the Persians in the east, through staging areas on the eastern Mediterranean coast.

What appealed to Constantine in choosing to favor Christianity was the churches' administrative coherence. Unlike the multiplicity of cults and practices that represented manifestations of the divine throughout the far-flung empire, the churches offered the possibility of creating an unprecedented unity in the state cult covering both west and east. The Christian churches, or church, were something new in the Mediterranean world: not one religion among many, but an ecclesiastical organization ready-made to match the basic administrative need of the state for unity. Christianity's intolerant exclusion of nonmembers required the suppression of other cults in its favor.

The bishops, with the autocrat's backing, worked miracles in purging the land; their imperial patron reaped the benefits in popularity with his subjects, especially along the Persian front where Christianity supplanted Mithraism, and in land and wealth seized from despoiled sanctuaries. Constantine ended up with a fifth of the arable land of the empire under his direct control: the biggest estate of all in an era of big estates. The wealth and prestige of the church itself were aligned with imperial power though controlled by its own bishops. The church sanctioned peace and order and explicitly enjoined submission to imperial jurisdiction, practicing a live-and-let-live policy with the new Rome, if not with other cults. In return the emperor allowed the clerics scope in the civil government, since Diocletian a function increasingly separate from the military.

Already rich and popular enough perhaps to have prevailed even without the emperor's favor, churches grew dramatically under imperial auspices. Cells and associations became major urban institutions, imperial in numbers, size, charitable donations, and display. Between 320 and 380, membership increased fivefold; Christian inscriptions, meager from the dangerous period before 312 and not attested between 312 and 350, proliferated after about 360. Seeing the miraculous reversal in the church's fortunes—bishops now in daily converse with the emperor—new members were eager to climb on the victorious bandwagon. In a society immobilized by Diocletian's organization of labor, the church offered one of the few avenues for advancement besides the army. Its mutual aid also replaced the social services formerly provided by urban cult institutions. Constantine's and the bishops' munificence, backed by threats of retribution on backsliders, produced mass conversions. The emperor forced minions to adopt the cult. Bishops organized missions to pacify people in or on the borders of their dioceses. Individuals proselytized, especially among barbarian captives of the empire. Monks and other ascetics made thousands of converts among rural workers and their families.

Constantine built church basilicas in great numbers and sizes all over the empire from Trier to Antioch, Jerusalem, and of course Constantinople. Basilicas were "royal halls" (from Greek *basileus*, "king"), used earlier for endorsed indoor markets, assemblies, and such; such churches enshrined royal values. Now that the church was for the first time officially entitled to own property, he gave hundreds of square miles of land as well as grain allowances to church-related institutions. All church land was exempt from taxes. With the land, thousands of workers and shepherds suddenly were added to the churches' charge, under ecclesiastical bailiffs, factors, and slave drivers. The churches also acquired private estates, as great lords became Christian in the wake of their master the emperor, and many of their lands found their way into the churches' endowment. By the end of the fourth century, people in Syria and Palestine commonly willed a third of their property to the church, removing it from the tax rolls and devoting it to the care of "widows," often the testators' own widows.

The growth of the church was particularly dramatic in Palestine. The emperor's mother Helena toured the land of the church's birth, visiting the caves, grottoes, and other modest saint shrines where Christians had congregated for the last two and a half centuries, marking the sites of Christ's birth and death and resurrection and other events in his life. Under her direction the Church of the Nativity in Bethlehem, the Church of the Annunciation in Nazareth, and the Church of the Holy Sepulcher in Jerusalem were founded, as well as the Church of the Beatitudes, the Church of the Transfiguration on Mount Tabor, and many more. Much of Jerusalem was rebuilt as an imperial city around the new church. Shrines such as St. Catharine's Monastery on Mount Sinai and the Church of Jacob's Well near Shechem commemorated Old Testament events, showing its use in Christian piety. Constantine's mother-in-law, Eutropia, asked him to abolish the cult of the Jewish shrine at Hebron and build a basilica there. The land was flooded with Christian pilgrims, who visited upward of at least thirty sites known to have been designated as shrines under imperial auspices, often rebuilt on earlier, more modest structures, even house churches. Excavation in the Church of the Holy Sepulcher has uncovered a fourth-century drawing in red and black of a Roman ship, with the inscription *Domine ivimus*, "O Lord, we came." In addition to the influx of aliens, the population of Palestine continued its growth, which during the Byzantine centuries reached a level not seen again until the end of the nineteenth century.

Constantine made clear his creed in an extant letter to the "inhabitants of the province of Palestine": those who follow the Christian religion, he observed, "are awarded with abundant blessings"; those who oppose it "have experienced results corresponding to their evil choice." During his reign he made sure this observation remained true. The disadvantage to the Jews of Palestine was at first slight, but before the end of the century horrid. Nonetheless, they began building basilica-like synagogues in Galilee, and the construction of synagogues continued through the rest of the biblical period.

Constantine needed to harness the administrative structure, the priesthood or episcopate, of his adopted cult to the administration of the empire and to reinforce its apparent unity. After moving the imperial capital away from Rome to the east, the emperor's design was to replace the Roman bishop, recognized in practice as head of the church, with a council of all bishops in unanimity, under his own sponsorship. (As the status of the eastern bishops rose, however, the bishop of Rome asserted his office in ways that later formed the basis of the papacy.) Within a year of the founding of his new capital, the emperor summoned the bishops of the empire to a great "ecumenical" ("covering the world": used of the church for the first time in this context) council in the town of Nicaea, just outside Constantinople. In 325, three hundred bishops with their princely entourages journeyed toward the capital at the emperor's expense, in an opulent display of the vindication of Christ's church against all opposition. There they were wined and dined in celebration of the earthly manifestation of Christ's kingdom.

To have a proper council, the bishops had to deal with a proper ostensibly theological question. A dispute that had begun in the church five years earlier over the views of Arius of Alexandria provided the occasion. Arius, who taught that Christ was not equal to God, but a semi-deified saint subordinate to God, was heir to the school of thought associated with the church in Antioch, rival to the Platonism of Alexandria. When a council led by the bishop of Alexandria expelled Arius in 321, he found sympathy and refuge with other Antiochans, notably Eusebius of Caesarea, who was about to become the chief court historian of the new emperor in his new capital. Besides presenting the emperor with the opportunity to

supervise the uniting of the divided church, the disagreement over
Arius's teaching raised an issue fundamental to a state cult adopted
precisely for its potential contribution to imperial oneness. The cult's
monotheism, belief in the oneness, or unity, of God, was in question.
According to the traditional Rule of Faith, one God was Father,
Son, and Holy Spirit, yet how could God be both one and three at
the same time?

The philosophical debate on the divinity of Christ, no doubt
prompted by questions that actually arose in the churches, veiled
a political debate over jurisdiction. The Christian church had abandoned the scriptures as law without replacing them with another
organized law. Under Constantine, was the episcopate to merge into
the legal form of the state to which it had been joined by the will
of the military dictator, or were the bishops to form their own legal
sphere? What kind of relationship was the emperor to have with
the entrenched ruling elite of his new cult? Was he the head of the
church or subject to it like any other Christian, the source of ecclesiastical law or subject to it? Could the emperor preempt the
right to appoint bishops, and thereby to control the disposition of
the snowballing wealth of the church? Now that the ruler of the
empire was Christian, was it any longer valid to make a distinction
between empire and church?

In addition to dealing with this issue directly, the bishops treated
it theologically, thus achieving nominal agreement with the emperor
where true unanimity was impossible. In the terms of the Arian
controversy, Arius's view of Jesus implied the subordination of the
church to the state, as the human Jesus was subordinate to God,
while the bishops' view made the church the equal of the state, as
Jesus was equal to God. Complete separation of church from state
was at that time inconceivable; cult was inherently linked to jurisdiction.

Arius stressed that God was one, and that Christ was subordinate
to God, rather than of the same quality of being, as it was put. The
Son was a created being; there was a time when he did not exist,
which could not be said of God. Others held that while God was
one he was also three, and that Christ was nothing less than God,
of the same being. At the Nicene council, under the eyes of the
emperor, their impressive new patron, the majority of bishops voted
in favor of the theory that Christ was of "same" being, not "like"
being, with God (thus *homoousios*). Nevertheless, since the matter
was more than theological, Arians continued to think what they

liked and understood the Nicene formula accordingly, and their opponents, who may be called the Catholics, did the same. At first the emperor himself was not sure of his own position.

In time the philosophical debate hardened into a series of rationalized answers to refined conundrums promulgated as the creeds of the imperial councils and taken as the standard of Christian exclusivity ever since. These showcased the schools of the church, especially that in Alexandria, the intellectual capital of the Hellenistic and Roman world, and gave intellectual clerics plenty to deal with in their struggles for position and favor in the new imperial church. Gregory of Nyssa mocked the persiflage: "If you ask for your change, someone philosophizes to you on the Begotten and Unbegotten. If you ask the price of bread, you are told, 'The Father is greater and the Son inferior.' If you ask, 'Is my bath ready?' someone answers, 'The Son was created from nothing.'" Meanwhile nearly the whole of what was actually in the scriptures was left off the official agenda.

As became clearer in the years following Nicaea, the Arian view implied as much about the status of the emperor as it said about the status of the Son of God. Arians regarded the eternal Logos, or Word (including rationality, the principle of law and order), as the means whereby God originally created order in the world. Order was to be created in the present through the imitation of the archetypical work of the Logos not by the historical Christ but by the emperor, the creator and guarantor of the order in which Christ's church itself had risen. Law and order were the prerogative of the emperor, the implementer of God's Logos, superseding Christ himself. The church's law and the emperor's law were one, and the emperor, as the preeminent interpreter of Logos virtually a divine savior in his own right, was the temporal head of the church. The court historian Eusebius, sympathetic with such views though not their prime exponent, put it in words that echo Josiah's call for unity against the traditional Judahite nobility: "Not two societies, church and state, but one God, one emperor, one religion," and a dutiful episcopate of one mind.

Arian views were especially popular with the new bureaucratic elite of the imperial church, supporters of its new administrative rationality and dependent on it for their appointments. Arians favored the unity of the empire: if the demigod Christ routed demons, the living and triumphant emperor would rout the demons of nationalism and dissension, curbing the cults that threatened to reduce the empire's coherence. Within ten years after Nicaea, toward the end of his life, Constantine had become an ardent supporter of the Arian party. His son Constantius (337–61), also an Arian, may even have believed himself to be the God-appointed head of the episcopate. Arianism succeeded largely as a result of the emperor's need to create a new cultic elite, loyal to the state, to replace the traditional elite whose influence he had escaped by moving to Constantinople. Arians were reluctant to make organizational decisions without imperial approbation. They were careful not to offend the emperor: one Arian writing, in quoting 1 Samuel 8 on the origin of royalty, left out verses 10–17, which detail the abuses of an emperor like Solomon, since they could apply equally well to Constantine and Constantius. In the view of many Arians, even the authority of the scriptures could be set aside by the authority of the emperor. For the church to control its Bible, an alternative view would have to prevail.

In contrast to the Arians, the Catholics construed the Logos primarily in terms of Christ's work of redemption in history, through the incarnation and the crucifixion and resurrection. The present embodiment of Christ's Logos was the church, as represented by the episcopate, whose status was assured by Christ's equality with God. The emperor, Catholics granted, was appointed by God to maintain social order, in imitation of creation, but this work of the Logos was by no means superior to the salvation revealed through Jesus Christ and then further through his extended body, the episcopate. The preeminent manifestation of the Logos lay in the eucharistic order, the heart of Christian cult, where the bishops exercised all prerogatives and the emperor none. The divine self-sacrifice of the historical Christ established the ecclesiastical law to which even a Christian emperor is subject.

During the course of the fourth century, Catholic views came to be favored by those concerned to protect the rights of the conservative episcopate from seizure by the crown. Catholics tended to be indigenous bishops, rather than imperial appointees, who regarded the suppression of Arians as a means of protecting the rights of their popular constituencies. Arians promoted the unity of the church, in line with imperial policy, around ambiguous credal formulas and the celebration of communion with all Christians. Catholics promoted its exclusivity, in the attempt to root out the Arian capitulation. They persisted in trying to spell out the correct definition of Christ's Godhood, even though they increasingly disliked empire-sponsored church councils. They refused communion to Arians, and justified this exclusion by stressing the historical succession of authority deriving through the bishops of the church from Peter, not Constantine. Was it not Peter to whom Christ had assigned the keys of the kingdom at the very moment he confessed him the Son of God? Indeed, the Catholic bishops traced their authority back to the priests and prophets of the Old Testament, whom kings were forced to obey. In this way the ancient tribal Israelite stance found its forum once again, the episcopal victory over the Marcionites was assured, and the Old Testament became an indispensable part of the Catholic charter of independence.

The foremost proponent of the Catholic position was Athanasius, a deacon and bishop's secretary at Nicaea who became bishop of Alexandria in 328. His outspoken resistance to the Arian tendency, seen as an attack on imperial unity, brought him into disfavor with the emperor and his episcopal supporters. In the struggle against opposition from Manichees and Meletians as well as Arians, Athanasius was ousted from his bishopric no less than five times, and by force of arms. Wielding scholarship, propaganda, and even physical intimidation by hired ruffians, eventually he prevailed, not least because he succeeded in uniting the wealthy Greek imperial city of Alexandria with the rest of Egypt in support of his views. His combination of Alexandrian Platonism with Coptic (Egyptian) social idealism laid the basis for the later rise of the see of Alexandria.

While Arianism was an urban movement, the followers of Bishop Meletius came from the Nile Valley and upper Egypt, especially from among those Coptic Christians who had suffered, as Meletius himself did, in the persecutions. Athanasius was able to win these areas from their attraction to Meletius's biblical literalism, populism, and severity on lapsed Christians by cultivating the support of the monks. He adopted ascetic practices himself, made friends with both Antony and Pachomius, the two great monastic leaders of Egypt, and wrote a popular pious life of Antony. While Antony and Athanasius disagreed on church order (Antony had no use for bishops, though he liked Athanasius personally), they agreed on the ideal of Christian life: martyrdom, or, as a substitute, an ascetic life in permanent combat against the forces of evil. Athanasius thus won the loyalty of the common people and monks of Egypt and Palestine: his view of Christ as fully God was just what they needed to help them fight their devils.

The Hebrew scriptures, if no longer the law, still remained the scriptures of the newly established church. What exactly they included became a subject of debate. Some Christian teachers of the fourth century, including Jerome, who translated the scriptures into Latin, declared that scriptures not in the Jewish canon, more or less fixed by the rabbis by the second century, were not of full authority, but could continue their wide use only for edification. Others, like Augustine, disagreed, and the circulation of these extra books in both Greek and Latin went on. At the end of the fourth century, a series of councils in Africa ruled with Rome's approval that the Old Testament consisted of the Jewish canon plus seven works: Wisdom, Ecclesiasticus, Baruch, Tobit, Judith, 1 and 2 Maccabees, along with the Greek additions to Esther and Daniel. Three other works, 1 and 2 Esdras plus the Prayer of Manasseh, since they were used widely, had enough official esteem to be included in Jerome's Vulgate. Jerome's position was taken up again by Protestants in the Reformation, when these books were isolated as the Apocrypha, "secreted things." The notion of canon, a standard or ruling, as applied to the Old and New Testaments as a list of writings became common in the imperial church of the second half of the fourth century. For example, the Council of Laodicea in 360 defined *ta akanonista biblia*, the noncanonical books, documents not allowed to be read in churches. The Greek word *kanon* came into Latin in the fourth century; Augustine used it frequently in reference to scriptures.

While Constantine's move to the east had deprived the see of Rome of some of its prestige, Christians in the Latin west continued to look to Rome and to Carthage in Africa for leadership. Africa produced the thinker whose theory confirmed Christian submission to secular authority. Augustine, namesake of the empire's founder, argued that humans do not have free will and thus overturned the previous Christian view that one could use one's free will in obedience to Christ's command rather than the state's.

The ultimate triumph of Christianity had to wait until the reign of Theodosius (378–395). Between him and the era of Constantine and Constantius, Julian (361–363) "the Apostate" reverted to Roman cults and projected the rebuilding of the Jewish temple, partly to gain Jewish support for war in Persia. When Valens (364–378), the last Arian emperor, died, Arianism was officially finished. Athanasius died in 373 on the eve of the victory of Catholicism.

By the Edict of Gratian in 380, Theodosius made Christianity the official cult of the empire. Published to the people of Constantinople soon after Theodosius's baptism, the edict later stood at the beginning of the Code of Justinian, the law of the Christian empire. Now the church in the empire became legally the church of the empire. Henceforth revolt against the church meant condemnation as a heretic by the law of the state; schismatics and sectaries, as rebels against the state, were deprived of civil rights regarding their legal status, property, testation, and assembly, and liable to fines, exile, and sometimes execution. Tertullian's dictum was ignored: "It is not the point of religion to compel religion." Catholic now meant not only universal (from Greek *katholos*, whole), but exclusive. In 381, the second ecumenical council, the Council of Constantinople, called by Theodosius to restore the Catholic Nicaean position after decades of Arian power under the emperors, decreed the divinity (political co-optation) of the Holy Spirit.

The corollary of Theodosius's edict was the abrogation of the toleration declared by the Edict of Milan. During 380–400 the church entered a new stage in the Christianization of the empire, as it mobilized armed force against its enemies, the non-Christians now declared without the law. Christian soldiers were recruited both from the mobs, who had already played a large role in the church's internal conflicts, and from imperial troops now at the church's disposal. Monks, bishops, generals, and emperors led the charge; heads of households and large landholders were urged, by persuasion and battery alike, to enforce the law on their dependents. Sanctioned as theological demonstration, pillaging was unleashed to convince the unconverted that only the Christian God could defend them from rapine and destruction. The missionary conversion of the empire was to be complete.

The imperial adoption of Christianity brought major changes for Jews and their scriptures. Even before Theodosius, under Constantius the Canons of Elvira had disallowed marriage between Christian and Jew and the holding of non-Jewish slaves by Jews. By law the property of anyone converting to Judaism was confiscated. The desire to assure that no future emperor would repeat Julian's short-lived apostasy led Julian's successors and others in the church more vigorously to oppose non-Christian cults, among which the Jewish cult was regarded as particularly odious. Forced conversions left Jews little recourse. In 404, under Theodosius's son Arcadius, Jews were forbidden to hold public office or serve in the

army, courts, or civil service of the empire. In 428 the Jewish patriarchate in Palestine was abolished altogether, and the political
center of Jewish life shifted to Persian Babylonia, breaking the pattern of Judean accommodation with Rome begun in the days of
the Hasmoneans. During this time the Jews became a minority in
Palestine for the first time.

To Jews, the Christian church was more than just another odd
imperial cult. The church claimed to be Israel, the church's victorious Messiah and episcopate the fulfillment of Old Testament
prophecy. With assistance from the emperor, a candidate for the
next Christian messiah, they now could back up their claim to sole
possession of the identity of Israel and of Israel's scriptures. The
church's arrogant and forceful preemption of basic Jewish claims
was a disaster for the Jews of Palestine.

The Jewish leaders of Palestine responded to these setbacks by
revising and elevating their understanding of Torah until the Torah
stood at the center of Jewish identity with an integrity to match that
of the newly victorious symbol of the Christian cross. The assumptions of the Mishnah were no longer adequate to the threat posed
by a Christian empire. Lightly regarded in the Mishnah, in midrash
Rome was framed as a dangerous sibling rival of the true Israel, an
Ishmael, Esau, or Edom. To counter the Christian messianic claims
of Byzantine power, the messiah was made the central aspect of the
Mishnah's complex Jewish hope: the messiah will come, as a rabbi,
embodying Torah. From a set of pronouncements on scriptural and
other topics illustrating an ongoing process of dealing with the
affairs of daily life, Torah grew into the critical principle of Jewish
life, the essential medium for the doctrine of Jewish salvation. Most
important, the Mishnah's authority, previously independent of
scripture, now required a clear and direct tie to the Hebrew scriptures that would displace the Christians' New Testament as the heir
to the written Torah.

During the fourth century, therefore, the practice of creating
midrash explicitly on the scrolls of Torah became more common.
In addition to the Tosefta, a collection of further rabbinic pronouncements unsystematically adding scriptural texts following the
Mishnah's order, the Sifra to Leviticus and Sifres to Numbers and
Deuteronomy were produced. These followed their scriptural base
rather than the order or organization of the Mishnah and provided
exegesis of scripture to back up positions taken in Mishnah. By the

middle of the fifth century, the Genesis Rabbah and Leviticus Rabbah had been produced, based on the mediating method of the
Palestinian Talmud and more propositional and philosophical than
the Sifra and Sifres. Reflecting a style of narrative interpretation
again common in the fourth century (and shared with the Gospels),
Genesis Rabbah reads Genesis as though it were the history of Rome
and Israel, equating Esau with Rome, Jacob with Israel.

About 400 a great supplemented version of the Mishnah incorporating the newer methods of structuring midrash according to
written Torah appeared as the Palestinian Talmud (*talmud*: com-
pendium of learning). It elaborated on thirty-nine of the fifty-two
tractates of Mishnah with paragraph-by-paragraph exegesis to explain the Mishnah, compare the Mishnah with Tosefta on the same
topic, and discuss theoretically the exegesis of scripture in light of
the Mishnah. The midrashic Gemara (added material) was in Aramaic. The Palestinian Talmud compromised between Pirke Aboth's
dispensing with scriptural citations altogether and the Sifra's and
Sifres' adherence to scripture's basic structure and rationale. It follows the Mishnah's order, but introduces arguments from scriptures
as in the midrash compositions. With the exception of one tractate,
this Talmud has no Gemara for the last two divisions, which deal
primarily with the temple: under the Christian empire after Julian,
it was quite out of the question.

The Palestinian Talmud and the Babylonian Talmud a century
or two later established the Mishnah alongside the Hebrew scriptures as principal sources of organization and legal principles, the
scripture for the Jews. Judaism thus came to rest on a dual Torah,
the written Torah of the scriptures and the oral Torah, also written
down, of the Mishnah. With their theory of Torah developed to
counter Christian imperialism, the Jewish leaders of Palestine established a mode of Judaism that could survive this crisis and others
to come with remarkable tenacity. The new Judaism quickly found
a home in the Persian realms, where it was supported as the Judaic
alternative to the Christian pretensions of Rome.

In addition to the written and oral Torahs, the Palestinian Talmud
identified a third kind of Torah, the living Torah. Fourth-century
midrash presented the rabbinic sage as Torah personified. The
saving knowledge of Torah was incarnate in the saving sage; what
the sage did was law. As the Torah expressed the rule of God, the
sage embodied the authority of the Torah. The Talmud's stories
about the sages' deeds and sayings in laying down the law, composed

by those very sages, confirmed their authority to do so, the authority of the Mishnah now being firmly anchored in the authority of scripture. The rabbis of the fourth century had achieved with the Torah what the bishops had done with the Old and New Testaments in the second century, that is, grounded themselves in a theory of personification of scriptural authority.

17

Lawful Powers

The empire now being firmly Christian and Catholic and rabbis alive and well in Persia, the story of the Bible's formation might be thought to have reached its happy ending. The organizations maintaining the Christian and Jewish scriptures, however, have yet to achieve full legal definition of their jurisdiction. The history of the Hebrew scriptures and their role in relating cult to jurisdiction can be rounded off only at the end of the sixth century with the formulation of the Code of Justinian and the Babylonian Talmud.

The fissure between east and west, Greek and Latin, within the Roman Empire, latent from the beginning, widened with the permanent division of administration in 395. When Rome fell to marauding migrant tribes in 476, the Byzantine east became the empire. There the boundaries were held by military strategy, diplomacy, and support from rural Christians at least until the mid-sixth century. Although the eastern empire was greatly reduced by the expansion of Islam through the Near East, Asia Minor, and the Balkans, Constantinople did not fall to Islam for another one thousand years, in 1453.

Two long and powerful reigns at the end of the biblical period, of Theodosius II (408–50) and Justinian (527–65, following a coregency with his uncle/adoptive father Justin), allowed the Byzantine Empire to prosper and expand, producing the greatest population Palestine was to see for over a thousand years. Agriculture was greatly improved in the east, including Palestine.

The Jewish population declined in Galilee, as many departed or converted under imperial threats of violence, and Theodosius abolished the patriarchate in Tiberias in 428. Many Jews moved to the

Golan, east of the Sea of Galilee, and there continued to build synagogues in the basilica style introduced under Constantine, but with simpler ornamentation than in previous centuries. On the eastern fringe of settlement, Jewish villages faded into Christian villages and monasteries.

The continuing effort to impose unity on the empire culminated in two great codifications of comprehensive law presented as Christian law, the Codex Theodosianus of 438 and the Codex Justinianus, second edition, of 534. The Christian empire, the power behind the Christian Bible, recognized by Constantine and established by Theodosius I, received its full legal definition in these codes.

In 435 Theodosius II ordered a commission to collect all the laws established by Constantine and his successors. The resulting codex published in 438 in sixteen books became a basis of a common law in the empire. Most of the edicts specifically on religion appear only in the last book; the bulk of the code deals with other, more comprehensive topics of law. (Among its provisions, Jews were ruled ineligible for public office.) The law therefore was not religious law but the codified law of the Christian empire, to which Christians as a matter of policy had always more or less deferred.

The few at the top of the church's hierarchy ranked high in the empire as well. By Justinian's time, the bishops of the five great sees, Rome, Constantinople, Alexandria, Antioch, and Jerusalem, known as the patriarchs, were on a par with senators, the wealthiest in the realm. Many bishops became extremely wealthy. The bishop of Rome received up to one quarter of the endowment income of his powerful see. These magnates were able to use the empire's authority to consolidate their power and back up their positions in intrachurch controversies.

One skilled in this kind of power politics was Augustine, whose view of human will as rebellious and sinful from birth, not able to do right but in awe of and dependent on higher authority, encouraged submission to imperial authority. The two cities in his *City of God* stood not for church and state, but for faith and unbelief, heaven and earth, an ideal church and city and an earthly church and city, the earthly city of unbelief being Babylon rather than Rome. Supported by the state in his polemics with opponents like the Donatists, Augustine contended that the existence of the heavenly order meant that Christians could leave the government of the mixed bag of good and evil in the world to properly constituted authorities. He manipulated the emperor into condemning Pelagius of Jerusalem, who accused the rich of using torture to maintain their power, by presenting Pelagius as a dangerous fomenter of social unrest.

During the reign of Theodosius II, pockets of resistance to episcopal authority were wiped out. The bishop of Edessa attacked the Marcionites in his city, demolished their meeting place, burned their scriptures, and confiscated all property for his church. His rules for church discipline included arraignment in chains before the city magistrate and execution for unreformed heretics, or traitors. The pro-imperial Theodoret from the same period wrote that eight whole Marcionite villages in his see were "converted," including thousands of Marcionites. Conversion meant terrorization, torture, and sometimes murder.

The work of unifying the imperial church was carried on in two more ecumenical, that is, imperial, councils summoned in 431 and 451. These were courts in which the assembled patriarchs, bishops, and secretaries with their factions put their views, particularly on the linked issues of unity and monotheism, before the emperor for his judgment.

At the first, in Ephesus in 431, Rome and Alexandria, the two great centers before Constantine, jointly attacked the upstart Constantinople in the person of its bishop Nestorius. The debating point chosen was not Nestorius's mild Pelagianism but the relation of the person of the Son of God to the person of Jesus Christ: were they separate and secondarily joined or an original fusion? Two persons or one? Nestorius said two, preserving the full humanity of Jesus, and thus precluding the use of the epithet "mother of God" for Mary (she could not be "mother of God" if Jesus was born before his merger with the Son of God). Nestorius's views found sympathy in Antioch, where he, like Arius, had studied, but offended devotees of the increasingly popular cult of Mary. His main adversary was Cyril, bishop of Alexandria (412–444), Athanasius's powerful see, who had continued the work of unifying the Egyptian church with pogroms against the Jews in Alexandria. A Platonist in the Alexandrian line of Origen, he held that Jesus was born Son of God, "begotten not made," two natures, one person. Cyril encouraged dissidence in Constantinople, bribed officials at court, won over the emperor's sister and wife, and finally persuaded Theodosius to call the showdown at Ephesus. Nestorius came with sixteen bishops on his side and an armed guard. Cyril brought fifty bishops as interested as ever in suppressing Arian tendencies and limiting the power of

Constantinople. The council duly condemned Nestorius, who fled to Persia. There, with official encouragement to defy the West, his followers established Nestorianism as the main form of Christianity in Persian lands. The Nestorian school in Edessa in Roman territory was shut down by the emperor in 489.

The defeat of Nestorius meant a triumph for the kind of exegesis of scripture inspired by Platonism that served to bolster authority. Nestorius's teacher in Antioch, Theodore of Mopsuestia, was the greatest of the Antiochan exegetes, committed to textual analysis, sticking to plain rather than allegorical meaning (although sometimes bringing the latter in through the back door), paying attention to historical context, taking note of evidence at hand, and questioning canonical writings. That is, he actually read the Bible, trying to take it on its own terms, and wrote critical reflections on most of it. Even though he was on good terms with Cyril despite Nestorius, his kind of interpretation was doomed to die out. The search for insight and authority being two different things, most of his writings were lost.

The second council saw a new alignment of Rome with Constantinople against overweening Alexandria. It made Jerusalem a patriarchate, and gave the bishop of Constantinople authority second only to the bishop of Rome, authority that the Roman bishop subsequently denied. The issue was carried over from Ephesus: how many natures did the two persons of the Son and Christ fused into one person imply, two or one? The Alexandrian Platonists and their popular following thought two natures were one too many to cover the fused person of the Ephesus formula. Christ's human nature, they said, was absorbed into his divine nature to make one. They were monophysites, or "one-nature-ites," opposed to what they called the malkites, or imperialists (*malk*: the "royal one"), the Catholic party sympathetic to the emperor. The Council of Chalcedon, sitting before the new emperor in Chalcedon right across the Bosporus from Constantinople, condemned the Alexandrian view and voted for the view of the bishop of Rome, that the two natures were perfectly united and distinct. With this contradiction fixed as the official or orthodox view, the struggle to define the empire's Christian unity that had started with Nicaea came to a close.

Like previous councils, Chalcedon contained its own seed of trouble. Only after Chalcedon defined Christ as fully human and fully divine could the policy and position of the emperor be called "imitation of Christ" rather than of God as *logos*. Once the emperor made this claim, the bishops had to decide whether to oppose this arrogation of incarnation. Were they the visible embodiment of Christ's authority on earth, or was the emperor? Here was the Arian controversy in a different guise, a continuing problem that went on well beyond the biblical period.

Justinian (527–65) spent the early years of his reign fighting in the west to reunite the eastern and western empires. Half successful in that effort, he turned to revitalizing his Stalin-like authority, whose sordid arrogance Procopius chronicled, in the east. A law commission appointed in 528 collected imperial laws going back as far as Hadrian, with most dating no earlier than Constantine, and incorporated them with the bulk of the edicts in Theodosius's code, sometimes with changes. The new code was published in a second edition approved in 534 and as a convenient Digest as well. Like Theodosius's code, Justinian's code consisted almost entirely of non-religious law, but, with the Edict of Gratian of 380 standing at its head, was even more emphatically the law of the Christian empire. It was to survive the collapse of Byzantine power before the Muslim onslaught as the definitive codification of Roman law.

While the empire had defined itself legally, the bishops' inter-pretation of scripture had not produced a scriptural law for them-selves. During the fourth through sixth centuries, the bishops created a canon law for the church, distinct though not separate from the state, assuming the laws pertaining to religion in Book 16 of Theodosius's code repeated in Justinian's code. Canon law dealt with the rules governing the organization that disposed of the churches' offices and endowment, under partial imperial direction. Based on Matthew's elevation of Peter, it provided for self-regulation of the episcopate under the bishop of Rome. The earliest compi-lations of rules were made in the east, starting with the rules, or canons, of the emperor's ecumenical council at Nicaea and adding those of local councils. For example, in Pontus Nicaean rulings were promulgated along with 25 canons of a council of Ankara in 314 and 15 canons of another council. By 451 over 150 canons had accumulated. These with the addition of the canons of Chalcedon and the 85 "Apostolic Canons" were translated into Latin and passed to the west in the fifth century. In the first half of the sixth century, the compilation was completed with the canonical letters of great bishops and some canons from Dionysius Exiguus, who had col-lected 400 canons mostly from African churches and councils and decretals (orders) of popes. Rome observed its own customs, along with the Nicaean canons, until it adopted Dionysius Exiguus and the Apostolic Canons. Thus a law for state and church, more alongside scriptures than out of scriptures, was finally established in the sixth century.

The church thrived on the wealth of the upper classes in Justinian's reign. Magnificent stone-built basilicas, adorned with rich mosaics, were erected, the grandest example being Hagia Sophia in Constantinople finished in 537 ("Solomon, I have outdone you"). Monasteries and over twenty bishoprics were established in the nondesert parts of Palestine. Most of these bishops were located in cities that grew up as administrative centers for the subsidized settlement of drylands, where big estates produced wine, dates, nuts, and spices for export—the food for the workers was shipped in from other parts of Palestine.

Monophysitism had become the common form of Christianity on the empire's frontiers among the people of Egypt, Syria, Armenia, and to a lesser degree Palestine. Monophysites' relations with the empire fluctuated. While they caused trouble for authority in the big cities, they also supported the one (emperor) against the many (magnates and bishops). Monophysite Axumites (in Ethiopia) and Arab tribes allied with the emperor protected Justinian's southeastern trade routes through Gaza to Elat and thence to the Indian Ocean, developed to bypass Persian control of the China silk route.

The most important of these sheikhs, the Ghassanids who controlled the Syrian desert and northwest Arabia, provided security for the southeastern region of the empire for fifty years, from 530 to 580, at a price. Justinian's wife, Theodora, a commoner and a monophysite, joined with a Ghassanid sheikh to prevail on Justinian to appoint a monophysite monk named Jacob as bishop of Edessa. Sharing a common language, Syriac, with the sheikhs and the Syrian people, Jacob was extremely effective in organizing popular monophysitism in wider Syria and Palestine, where monophysite Jacobites exist to this day.

Faced with continuing hostilities along his Persian and German frontiers fomented by his own aggression, Justinian also had to contend with unrest among urban mobs and especially the rural populace in southern Asia Minor, the monophysite masses. Popular discontent, rooted in economic hardship, distant imperial government, and domination by Greek foreigners, was manipulated by the ambitious to back their bids for power. Leaders bent on church

careers rallied the crowds around theological slogans and adver-
tisement of superior asceticism, luring the superstitious with promises of better life, to believe that their salvation depended on the
correct answer to some philosophical conundrum the leader had
resolved. The alliance between monophysites and the imperial state
ended when Justin II, Justinian's successor, closed the monophysite
churches and imprisoned their bishops and priests. The empire
thus destroyed one of its own bulwarks and drove the suppressed
monophysites to welcome the Muslims in the seventh century.

Meanwhile in Persia, Constantine's contemporary Shapur II and
his successors busily persecuted Christians, and the large Judean
community in Babylonia (Mesopotamia) was cultivated by Persian
rulers as a counter to Roman expansion of control over the Palestinian Judean leadership. After 70, when the fall of the temple
severed Judeans from that source of authority, the Persians created
their own Judean leader out of the "head of the deportation" (hark-
ing back to the Babylonian exile), or exilarch, a nonpharisee who
claimed descent from the house of David through the male line
superior to the Hillels' descent through the female line. The exilarch
with his armed retinue collected taxes and preserved order on behalf
of his Persian masters. As early as the second century the exilarch
presented himself as a restored Davidid, a monarch established by
the empire (more successfully than in 520 B.C.E.) who ruled as a
surrogate for the messiah. By the third century he could use Persian
and personal law to judge cases in his own courts, even against the
rabbis—a position comparable to the relationship of Christians to
imperial law gained only in the fourth century.

The rabbinic school established in Babylonia by refugees from
the Bar Kosiba war in Palestine formed the second focus of authority
among Babylonian Judeans. As head of the community, the exilarch
provided the rabbis' finances and in return used rabbis as retainers
to enhance his traditional authority over against assimilated Judean
opponents, the Persianized Judean elite. The exilarch's court supported the Mishnah when it first came to Babylonia, but rabbis
ruled from it only with the exilarch's permission. The learned rabbis
who knew not only the whole Torah but also the secrets of creation,
miracles, astrology, medicine, magic, and practical religion, posed
a threat even to the Persian magi and countered the exilarch's authority with their own legal tradition in oral law. They had little use
for the exilarch's presumption, especially before they themselves
exalted the messiah as the focus of resistance to the empire.

The split between rabbis and exilarch came in the fourth century, over whether rabbis should pay taxes. They had not in Palestine under the Romans, and they enjoyed other privileges in the Persian court and markets and the exilarch's court. But in Babylonia the exilarch was the Persian tax farmer for Judeans. Although reluctant to ask for aid against the rabbis from the otherwise occupied Persian military, for fear of making martyrs of the rabbis as well as the persecuted Christians, the exilarchs seem to have managed to collect a poll tax on all Judeans. Nevertheless rabbinic prestige grew along with attendance at their schools. Already by the fourth century, the rabbis had supplanted the exilarch in issuing the calendar rules in accordance with Palestinian usage. Eventually they followed the Palestinian rabbis into sympathy with the exilarch's messianic views.

These views brought the wrath of the Persians on both parties in the fifth century, when messianic fervor among Jews spurred the empire to wipe out Jewish government altogether. The Persian reaction, possibly fired by conflict between magi and rabbis, came to a head in 468, called in the Babylonian Talmud "the year of the destruction of the world." In its aftermath, the scholarly class, despite its implication in the uprisings, rose to exclusive leadership among Babylonian Jews. The exilarchate was not to be revived until the Muslim conquest. Babylonian rabbis also enjoyed prestige in Palestine: about 520 the rabbi Mar Sutra from Babylonia established a line of seven generations as heads of the Jews in Tiberias, until the main school moved to Jerusalem in the eighth century. After the establishment of Christianity in the West by Theodosius I and II, Babylonia became the focus of Jewish life.

Under these conditions, Babylonian Jews made their own additions to the Mishnah, following the model of the Palestinian Talmud, in the years 550–600. This enormous Babylonian Talmud also includes extensive exegesis of passages from both Mishnah and scriptures. Thirty-seven of the Mishnah's fifty-two tractates, including those on the practical regulation of the temple cult not dealt with in the Palestinian Talmud, are covered. The Babylonians followed the Sifra and Sifres in organizing long sections of discourse not around the Mishnah tractate, as was largely the case in the Palestinian Talmud, but around a biblical passage or book.

Under the influence of narrative midrash, the Babylonian Talmud carried the representation of the Torah in the rabbinic sage to its eventual conclusion, the representation of God as a rabbinic sage. Its stories of the sages, like the stories about Jesus in the Gospels, represented the rule, power, and authority of God personified and interacting in a saving way with humans. So Jews in the fifth and sixth centuries used the same form of midrash in writings that were to become official as did the Christians of the first century in what became their official writings, the New Testament.

With no rival critique of Judaism to counter and no rival theory of incarnation to avoid, the step from Torah as incarnate in the sage to God as incarnate in the sage was taken in Persian Babylonia not in Roman Palestine. In the West the bishops had preempted the right to represent God's incarnation through embodied tradition and Jesus. Both organizations, the rabbis and the bishops, had established the authority of the authorities maintaining their scriptures; both were divine. The Hebrew temple scriptures were irrevocably bound as codices, as a book and books as we know them. The Bible had come into being.

18

Sequel

The Bible was produced by demands for legitimacy following changes in rule—from David's usurpation, through Jeroboam, Jehu, and Josiah, the Persians, Aaronids, Hasmoneans, and Herodians, finally to the Romans and the Byzantine emperors and their ecclesiastical clerics. The turning points in its history have been the building of the temple, the restoration of the temple under the Persians, the destruction of the temple by the Romans, the re-creation of temples by Constantine, and the legal canonizations: Roman law, the churches' canon law, and the Babylonian Talmud. The Romans have dominated the second half of the history: they helped re-create the Judean state, conquered it, destroyed it, then accommodated and supported its two main offshoots, until one of those became the Roman cult. That one survived the empire to become in the West in the twelfth and thirteenth centuries an empire of sorts in its own right, the papal state of the high Middle Ages.

The story of the scriptures' relation to worldly jurisdiction does not end with the codification of the rabbinic and episcopal organizations' laws and the Roman imperial law as Christian law. The papal revolution, Reformation, and republican secularization in the industrial era all added new episodes, and the same issues live on to the present.

In 800 the Roman church in the West allied with the dictator Charlemagne to re-create the Holy Roman Empire. In the eleventh to the thirteenth centuries, starting with Pope Gregory VII, the church itself, with the invaluable if inconsistent support of Norman and French rulers, became a state. Canon law became the basis of

a total state apparatus and assumed its prerogatives. This state lives
on in the Vatican state, whose wealth spans the world. The uniting
of church law and mundane power forced other states to define
their law separate from the church rather than in conjunction with
the church, since the church was now its own state. This is the origin
of the distinction between church and state as we know it, with its
legal definition of the secular state as distinct from the church. From
this we also derive our notion of "religion" as a private matter
separate and distinct from the state. Under these circumstances,
Jews as heirs to a different accommodation of scripture to jurisdiction continued to suffer hardship in the West and were periodically
expelled from states, their devastation at Christian hands coming
in the twentieth century.

When the Persian and the better part of the Byzantine realms
became Muslim in the seventh century, Islam, itself influenced by
the Bible, created a monarchic theocracy, under which Christians
and Jews were tolerated as peoples with their own laws based on
scriptures Muslims respected. Jewish law continued its process of
definition under Islam, especially in the work of scholars in the
eleventh and twelfth centuries. In the Christian eastern sphere the
Orthodox church, which split from the Roman church in the eleventh century, evolved into several national churches based on the
use of vernacular languages as opposed to Latin. With the fall of
Constantinople in 1453, its leadership diffused and preeminence
passed for a time to the Russian church.

The Roman church fragmented in the Reformation of the sixteenth century. New kinds of bonds were formed between secular
states and churches that named the Bible as their principal authority
and again condoned its reading among the masses. New states broke
free of big power coalitions cemented by the power of the church
and linked themselves with new anti-Roman churches. The church's
lands were seized for rulers and nobilities. The great powers, the
Habsburgs and France, remained Catholic. Religion in the new
Protestant states became a personal matter. Even the Calvinist international, the staunchest attempt to re-create unity among the
new churches, faded in the face of states' pride.

The Orthodox churches that were tolerated in Islam formed the
basis of various nationalist movements in the nineteenth century,
much as Reformation churches had done in the sixteenth. With
British and other Western aid, the new Greek state became the

center of the Greek church, one among several such national centers. Thus with the exception of the Roman Catholic church nearly all Christian churches are now defined administratively in terms of their congruence with a secular state.

The congruence of Christian churches with separate secular states had a profound influence on Judaism in the modern era. Inspired by nationalist movements and reacting to the treatment of Jews in Russia and eastern Europe, Jews in the West developed Zionism, a nonmessianic, soon socialist, political movement that led to the creation of the Jewish state, a refuge from persecution, again with the essential aid of the empires, Britain and the United States, at the cost of Palestinian integrity. Zionists adopted a liberal republican model of the state, with state and Torah separate. A nonreligious Jewish state, possible for Judaism only by following the Reformation pattern in republican form, is an innovation currently transforming Judaism as much as did the events of 70 or 313. Where Jews understand their identity in terms of the state as well as Torah, a secularized Judaism may emerge, a Jewish civil religion previously unknown.

Thus in many Protestant and Orthodox states (prior to modern communist takeovers), and in the Vatican and Zionist Israel, Christians and Jews have re-created the state-level jurisdiction, or relatives thereof, lost with the temple. While the law of such states has little to do with what is in the Bible, their claim to legitimacy has much to do with the Bible.

Chronology

Political
Literary

1300 B.C.E.

Tribal Israel achieved power
Rameses II (ruled about 1279-1212)
Merenptah (ruled about 1212-1202)

1200

Settlement expansion in Palestine began
Rameses III (ruled about 1183-1152)
Philistines ruled in lowland cities

1100

War songs of Israel
Saul

1000

David (early tenth century)
    Davidic royal defense of and against usurpation: court apolo-
        gies in Samuel
    Royal cult histories: Ark narrative in Samuel; J
    Royal cult prayers: psalms of David
Solomon, coup d'état under Davidic palace guard (mid to late
        tenth century)
Temple built (about 950)
    Royal additions to court apologies: beginning of 1 Kings
    Royal sayings collection: proverbs
    Royal additions to cult prayers and songs

Jeroboam I, revolt of Israel against house of David (late tenth
    century)
Israelite royal additions to J: E
900
Omri (ruled about 883-872)
Ahab (ruled about 872-851)
Elijah
Elisha
Joram, son of Ahab, paid tribute to Shalmaneser III of Assyria
    (841)
Jehu, coup d'état against house of Omri (ruled about 839-812)
Athaliah, Omrid queen mother, ruled Judah (about 839-833)
    Israelite royal defense of usurpation: Elijah and Elisha nar-
    ratives
    Revision of court apologies to reflect saints' roles
Joash of Judah (ruled about 833-794)
Joahaz (ruled about 812-796)
800
Joash of Israel (ruled about 796-781)
Amaziah of Judah (ruled about 794-766)
Jeroboam II (ruled about 781-745)
Uzziah/Azariah of Judah (ruled about 781-747)
Jotham of Judah (ruled about 748-734)
Tiglath-pileser III (ruled 745-727)
    Amos
Menahem (ruled about 745-736)
Peqah (ruled about 735-732)
Ahaz of Judah (ruled about 734-715)
Hosea (ruled about 732-724)
    Hosea (saint)
Shalmaneser V (ruled 727-722)
Fall of Samaria (722)
Sargon II (ruled 722-705)
Merodach-baladan (ruled 721-710, 703)
    Micah
    Isaiah
Hezekiah (ruled about 715-687)
    Additions to royal collection of proverbs
Sennacherib (ruled 705-681)
Assyrian siege of Jerusalem (701)

700
Manasseh (ruled about 696-642)
Esarhaddon (ruled 681-669)
Ashurbanipal (ruled 669-627)
Josiah (about 640-609)
    Temple repair, royal history of house of David and its temple,
        Dtr 1 (about 622)
    Revision of saints' divans, particularly Isaiah and Amos
Necho II (ruled 610-595)
    Jeremiah
Nabopolassar (ruled 626-605)
    Zephaniah
Fall of Ashur (614)
Fall of Nineveh (612)
    Nahum
Jehoiakim (ruled 609-598)
Battle of Carchemish (605)
Nebuchadrezzar (ruled 605-562)
600
Jehoiachin (ruled 598-562 at least, almost entirely in exile)
Fall of Jerusalem, deportation of house of David (598)
Zedekiah (ruled 598-587)
    Habakkuk
    Ezekiel
Fall of Jerusalem, destruction of Davidid temple, second court
        deportation (587)
Gedaliah (governed 587-586)
    Revision of Josianic temple history, Dtr 2 (about 560-550)
    Revision of Amos divan
    Jonah
    Revision of Micah divan
    Revision of Jeremiah divan
Nabonidus (ruled 555-539)
Cyrus (ruled 559-530)
Fall of Babylon to Cyrus (539)
    Revision of Isaiah divan, Second Isaiah
Sheshbazzar
Cambyses (ruled 530-522)
Egypt falls to Persians (525)
Zerubbabel
    Revision of Hezekiah's JE by Aaronid priests: P

Darius (ruled 521-486)
Rebuilding of Davidid temple (about 520-515)
  Haggai
  Zechariah 1-8
  Lamentations, temple lament psalms
500
  Battle of Marathon (490)
  Xerxes (ruled 486-465)
  Battle of Salamis (480)
    Revision of Davidic temple psalms
    Revision of Zechariah divan (Zech. 9-14)
    Malachi
  Artaxerxes (ruled 464-425)
  Egyptian revolt against Persia (460-455)
  Ezra (governed about 458-?)
  Peace of Kallias (448)
  Nehemiah (governed about 445-432)
    Revision of Isaiah divan, Third Isaiah
    Chronicles (probably multiple editions)
    Ezra, Nehemiah
    Joel
    Obadiah
    Esther
    Ruth
    Job
400
  Campaigns of Alexander of Macedon (336-323)
  Seleucus I Nicator (ruled 305-281)
    Canticles
300
  Ptolemy II of Egypt (283-246)
  Antiochus I Soter of Syria (ruled 281-260)
  Antiochus II Theos (ruled 260-246)
  Ptolemy III (ruled 246-221)
  Seleucus II Callinicus (ruled 245-226)
  Antiochus III (ruled 223-187)
  Simon II, high priest (ruled about 220-190)
    Ecclesiastes
200
    Ben Sira (Ecclesiasticus) (about 190)
  Onias III, high priest (ruled about 190-175)

Roman victory at Magnesia (188)
Seleucus IV (ruled 187-175)
Antiochus IV Epiphanes (ruled 175-164)
Jason, high priest (about 175-172)
Menelaus, high priest (172-162)
    Daniel (165)
Maccabees captured Jerusalem (164)
Demetrius I Soter (ruled 162-150)
Alcimus, high priest (162-159)
Jonathan Maccabeus (ruled 161-142)
Jonathan high priest (152)
Alexander Balas (ruled 150-145)
Simon Maccabeus (ruled 142-134)
John Hyrcanus (ruled 134-104)
    2 Maccabees
    Tobit?
Aristobulus I (ruled 104-103)
Alexander Janneus (ruled 103-76)
100
    1 Maccabees
    Judith
Salome Alexandra (ruled 76-67)
Aristobulus II (ruled 67-63)
Pompey captured Jerusalem (63)
Hyrcanus II, high priest (63-40)
Triumvirate ruled Rome (43-36)
Parthian capture of Jerusalem (40)
Antigonus II, high priest and king (40-37)
Herod appointed king of Judeans by Roman senate (39, ruled
    37-4)
Octavian (Augustus) ruled Rome as sole emperor (27 B.C.E.-14
    C.E.)
Herod began reconstruction of temple (18)
    Additions to temple psalms
Herod Antipas, tetrarch (4 B.C.E.-39 C.E.)
Philip, tetrarch (4 B.C.E.-34 C.E.)
1 C.E.
Hillel, Shammai
Tiberius (ruled 14-37)
Pontius Pilate (governed 26-36)
Jesus of Nazareth

Caligula (ruled 37-41)
Claudius (ruled 41-54)
Agrippa I, king of Judeans (ruled 41-44)
    Letters of Paul
Agrippa II, king of expanding parts (beginning 49)
Nero (ruled 54-68)
Paul's arrest in Jerusalem (58)
    Letters of Paul
First Judean war (66-70)
Vespasian conquered Galilee (67) and Perea and parts of Judea
    (68)
Year of four emperors (68-69)
Vespasian (ruled 69-79)
Fall of Jerusalem, destruction of temple (70)
    Mark
Johanan ben Zakkai (primacy about 72-80)
Josephus wrote *Judean War* (about 75)
Titus (ruled 79-81)
Gamaliel II (primacy about 80-120)
    Last additions to psalms
Domitian (ruled 81-96)
    Matthew, Luke-Acts, John
    Revelation, other New Testament letters
Trajan (ruled 98-117)
    Didache
100
Hadrian (ruled 117-138)
    Barnabas (about 130)
Second Judean, or Bar Kosiba (Kochba), war (132-135)
Antoninus Pius (ruled 138-161)
Marcion (worked about 140-160)
    Diognetus (about 150)
Justin Martyr wrote two apologies (about 155, 160)
Montanism
Marcus Aurelius (ruled 161-180)
Rabbi Judah (about 170-220)
Montanist movement in Phrygia (172)
Irenaeus made bishop of Lyon (178)
Clement of Alexandria (worked about 180-200)
Irenaeus wrote *Against Heresies* (about 185)
Septimius Severus (ruled 193-211)

Compilation of Mishnah
200
Origen (worked about 210-253)
Severus Alexander, last of Severan dynasty (ruled 222-235)
Decius (ruled 249-251)
  Pirke Aboth (about 250)
Valerian (ruled 253-260)
Gallienus (ruled 253-268) ended persecution of Christians (260),
    issued rescript (261)
Aurelian (ruled 270-275)
Judah Nesiah, patriarch
Diocletian (ruled 284-305)
300
Constantine (ruled 307-337)
Constantine saw sign of victorious cross at Mulvian Bridge (312)
Edict of Milan (313)
Constantine sole emperor (324)
Council of Nicaea (325)
Founding of Constantinople (330)
Constantius (ruled 337-360)
Council of Laodicea (360)
Julian (ruled 360-363)
Death of Athanasius (373)
Theodosius I (ruled 378-395)
Edict of Gratian
Division of Roman Empire (395)
400
  Palestinian Talmud
Theodosius II (ruled 408-450)
Augustine wrote *City of God* (411-426)
Jewish patriarchate abolished (428)
  Tosefta, Sifra, Sifres
Augustine's death (430)
Council of Ephesus (431)
Theodosius' code (438)
  Genesis Rabbah
Council of Chalcedon (451)
Persecution of Jews in Babylonia (468)
Fall of Rome (476)
500
Justinian (ruled 527-565)

Justinian's code, first edition (528-529)
Justinian closed schools in Athens (529)
Justinian code, second edition (534)
Justinian completes Hagia Sophia (537)
  Babylonian Talmud (about 550)

Selected Reading

1. What Is the Bible?

Norman K. Gottwald, *The Hebrew Bible: A Socio-Literary Introduction*, Philadelphia: Fortress Press, 1985.

John H. Hayes and J. Maxwell Miller, eds., *Israelite and Judaean History*, Philadelphia: Westminster Press, 1977.

Kathleen M. Kenyon, *The Bible and Recent Archaeology*, rev. ed. by P. R. S. Moorey, Atlanta: John Knox Press, 1987.

J. Maxwell Miller and John H. Hayes, *A History of Ancient Israel and Judah*, Philadelphia: Westminster Press, 1986.

Martin Jan Mulder, ed., *Mikra: The Interpretation of the Hebrew Bible in Judaism and Early Christianity*, Philadelphia: Fortress Press, 1988.

2. People of Palestine

Oded Borowski, *Agriculture in Iron Age Israel*, Winona Lake, Ind.: Eisenbrauns, 1987.

Elihu Grant, *The Peasants of Palestine*, New York: Pilgrim Press, 1907.

David C. Hopkins, *The Highlands of Canaan: Agricultural Life in the Early Iron Age*, Sheffield: Almond Press, 1985.

John Kautsky, *The Politics of Aristocratic Empires*, Chapel Hill: University of North Carolina Press, 1982.

Ludwig Koehler, *Hebrew Man*, London: SCM Press, 1956.

Gerhard Lenski, *Power and Privilege: A Theory of Social Stratification*, Chapel Hill: University of North Carolina Press, 1984.

Gideon Sjoberg, *The Preindustrial City: Past and Present*, New York: The Free Press, 1960.

3. Israel Before the Bible

Robert B. Coote, *Early Israel: A New Horizon*, Minneapolis: Fortress Press, forthcoming.

Israel Finkelstein, *The Archaeology of the Israelite Settlement*, Jerusalem: Israel Exploration Society, 1988.

Baruch Halpern, *The Emergence of Israel*, Chico: Scholars Press, 1983.

Kenneth A. Kitchen, *Pharaoh Triumphant: The Life and Times of Ramesses II, King of Egypt*, Warminster: Aris & Phillips, 1982.

4. David Begins the Bible

Walter Brueggemann, *David's Truth*, Philadelphia: Fortress Press, 1985.

Robert B. Coote and David Robert Ord, *The Bible's First History*, Minneapolis: Fortress Press, 1989.

P. Kyle McCarter, "The Apology of David," *Journal of Biblical Literature* 99 (1980): 489–504.

————, " 'Plots, True or False'—The Succession Narrative as Court Apologetic," *Interpretation* 35 (1981): 355–67.

5. Solomon and the Temple

Menahem Haran, *Temples and Temple-Service in Ancient Israel*, Oxford: Clarendon Press, 1978.

Christian E. Hauer, Jr., "The Economics of National Security in Solomonic Israel," *Journal for the Study of the Old Testament* 18 (1980): 63-73.

Tryggve N. D. Mettinger, *Solomonic State Officials: A Study of the Civil Government Officials of the Israelite Monarchy*, Lund: Gleerup, 1971.

Peter J. Taylor, *Political Geography:* World Economy, Nation-State *and Locality,* Harlow: Longman, 1985, 1989.

6. Revolution in Israel

Robert B. Coote, *In Defense of Revolution: The Elohist's History*, Minneapolis: Fortress Press, forthcoming.

————, ed., *Elijah and Elisha in Socioliterary Perspective*, Semeia Studies, Decatur: Scholars Press, forthcoming.

7. Great Estates

Joseph Blenkinsopp, *A History of Prophecy in Israel from the Settlement in the Land to the Hellenistic Period*, Philadelphia: Westminster Press, 1984.

Marvin L. Chaney, "Bitter Bounty: The Dynamics of Political Economy Critiqued by the Eighth-Century Prophets," in Robert L. Stivers, ed., *Reformed Faith and Economics*, Lanham, Maryland: University Press of America, 1989, 15-30.

Robert B. Coote, *Amos among the Prophets: Composition and Theology*, Philadelphia: Fortress Press, 1981.
Bernhard Lang, "The Social Organization of Peasant Poverty in Biblical Israel," *Journal for the Study of the Old Testament* 24 (1982): 47–63.
A. Leo Oppenheim, *Ancient Mesopotamia: Portrait of a Dead Civilization*, rev. ed., Chicago: University of Chicago Press, 1977.
D. N. Premnath, "Latifundialization and Isaiah 5:8–10," *Journal for the Study of the Old Testament* 40 (1988): 49–60.

8. The Iron Empire

Richard Elliott Friedman, *Who Wrote the Bible?* New York: Summit Books, 1987.
Nadav Na'aman, "Hezekiah's Fortified Cities," *Bulletin of the American Schools of Oriental Research* 261 (1986): 5–21.
Jonathan Rosenbaum, "Hezekiah's Reform," *Harvard Theological Review* 72 (1979): 23–43.

9. Josiah and the Deuteronomists

Marvin L. Chaney, "Joshua," in Bernhard Anderson, ed., *The Books of the Bible*, New York: Charles Scribner's Sons, 1989, 103–12.
W. Eugene Claburn, "The Fiscal Basis of Josiah's Reforms," *Journal of Biblical Literature* 92 (1973): 11-22.
Richard D. Nelson, *The Double Redaction of the Deuteronomistic History*, Sheffield: JSOT Press, 1981.

10. Babylonian Rulers and the Court in Exile

Peter R. Ackroyd, *Exile and Restoration: A Study of Hebrew Thought of the Sixth Century B.C.*, Philadelphia: Westminster Press, 1968.
Robert B. Coote and David Robert Ord, *Creation in Seven Days: The Priestly History*, Minneapolis: Fortress Press, forthcoming.
Richard Elliott Friedman, *The Exile and Biblical Narrative: The Formation of the Deuteronomistic and Priestly Works*, Chico: Scholars Press, 1981.
Ralph W. Klein, *Israel in Exile: A Theological Interpretation*, Philadelphia: Fortress Press, 1979.
D. J. Wiseman, *Nebuchadrezzar and Babylon*, Oxford: Oxford University Press, 1985.

11. Persian Rulers and the New Temple

Joseph Blenkinsopp, *Prophecy and Canon: A Contribution to the Study of Jewish Origins*, South Bend, Ind.: Notre Dame University Press, 1977.
———, "The Mission of Udjahorresnet," *Journal of Biblical Literature* 106 (1987): 409–21.

Eric M. Meyers, "The Shelomith Seal," *Eretz Israel* 18 (1985): 33*–38*.
James A. Sanders, *Torah and Canon*, Philadelphia: Fortress Press, 1972.
Morton Smith, *Palestinian Parties and Politics that Shaped the Old Testament*,
New York: Columbia University Press, 1971, 1987.

12. Greek Rulers and Rome's Hasmoneans

John Corbett, "The Pharisaic Revolution and Jesus as Embodied Torah,"
Sciences religieuses/Studies in Religion 15 (1986): 375–91.
Erich S. Gruen, *The Hellenistic World and the Coming of Rome*, Berkeley:
University of California Press, 1984.
A. H. M. Jones, *The Greek City from Alexander to Justinian*, Oxford: Oxford
University Press, 1940.
E. Rivkin, *A Hidden Revolution*, Nashville: Abingdon Press, 1978.
G. E. M. de Ste. Croix, *The Class Struggle in the Ancient Greek World: From
the Archaic Age to the Arab Conquest*, Ithaca: Cornell University Press,
1981.
William Tarn, *Hellenistic Civilization*, 3d ed., rev. by G. T. Griffith, London:
Edward Arnold, 1952.
Victor Tcherikover, *Hellenistic Civilization and the Jews*, New York: Jewish
Publication Society of America, 1959.

13. Roman Rulers, Herodians, and the End of the Temple

Peter Garnsey and Richard Saller, *The Roman Empire: Economy, Society and
Culture*, Berkeley: University of California Press, 1987.
Martin Goodman, *The Ruling Class of Judaea: The Origins of the Jewish Revolt
Against Rome* A.D. *66–70*, Cambridge: Cambridge University Press,
1987.
Richard J. Horsley, *Jesus and the Spiral of Violence*, San Francisco: Harper
& Row, 1987.
Douglas E. Oakman, *Jesus and the Economic Questions of His Day*, Lewiston,
New York: Edwin Mellen Press, 1986.
Antony J. Saldarini, *Pharisees, Scribes, and Sadducees in Palestinian Society: A
Sociological Approach*, Wilmington: Michael Glazier, 1988.
Elisabeth Schüssler-Fiorenza, *In Memory of Her: A Feminist Theological Re-
construction of Christian Origins*, New York: Crossroad, 1985.
Alan F. Segal, *Rebecca's Children: Judaism and Christianity in the Roman World*,
Cambridge: Harvard University Press, 1986.
Geza Vermeś, *Jesus the Jew: A Historian's Reading of the Gospels*, London:
Collins, 1973.

14. Old Scriptures, New Jurisdictions

Everett Ferguson, *Backgrounds of Early Christianity*, Grand Rapids: Wm. B.
Eerdmans, 1987.

Harry V. Gamble, *The New Testament Canon: Its Making and Meaning*, Philadelphia: Fortress Press, 1985.

Robert M. Grant, *Augustus to Constantine: The Rise and Triumph of the Christian Movement into the Roman World*, San Francisco: Harper and Row, 1990.

Robert Kirschner, "Apocalyptic and Rabbinic Responses to the Destruction of 70," *Harvard Theological Review* 78 (1985): 27–46.

Bruce Metzger, *The Canon of the New Testament: Its Origin, Development, and Significance*, Oxford: Oxford University Press, 1987.

Jacob Neusner, *First-Century Judaism in Crisis: Yohanan ben Zakkai and the Renaissance of Torah*, New York: KTAV, 1982.

———, Peder Borgen, Ernest S. Frerichs, and Richard Horsley, eds., *The Social World of Formative Christianity and Judaism*, Philadelphia: Fortress Press, 1988.

Raphael Patai and Jennifer Patai, *The Myth of the Jewish Race*, rev. ed., Detroit: Wayne State University Press, 1989.

E. P. Sanders, ed., *Jewish and Christian Self-Definition, vol. 1, The Shaping of Christianity in the Second and Third Centuries*, Philadelphia: Fortress Press, 1980.

———, A. I. Baumgarten, and Alan Mendelson, eds., *Jewish and Christian Self-Definition, vol. 2, Aspects of Judaism in the Graeco-Roman Period*, Philadelphia: Fortress Press, 1981.

Klaus Wengst, *Pax Romana and the Peace of Jesus Christ*, Philadelphia: Fortress Press, 1988.

15. Rabbis and Bishops in the Empire

Hans von Campenhausen, *The Formation of the Christian Bible*, Philadelphia: Fortress Press, 1972.

P. R. Coleman-Norton, *Roman State and Christian Church: A Collection of Legal Documents to A.D. 535*, 3 vols., London: SPCK, 1966.

John H. Elliott, "Patronage and Clientism in Early Christian Society," *Foundations and Facets Forum* 3, 4 (December 1987): 39–48.

Martin Goodman, *State and Society in Roman Galilee, A.D. 132–212*, Totowa, N.J.: Rowman & Allanheld, 1983.

Paul Johnson, *A History of Christianity*, New York: Atheneum, 1976.

Jacob Neusner, *Invitation to Midrash*, Philadelphia: Fortress Press, 1989.

Lawrence H. Schiffmann, *Who Was a Jew? Rabbinic and Halakhic Perspectives on the Jewish-Christian Schism*, New York: KTAV, 1985.

Daniel Sperber, *Roman Palestine 200–400, the Land: Crisis and Change in Agrarian Society as Reflected in Rabbinic Sources*, Ramat Gan: Bar-Ilan University Press, 1978.

16. Constantine's Christian Triumph

G. T. Armstrong, "Imperial Church Building and Church State Relations, A.D. 313–363," *Church History* 36 (1967): 3–17.

David Weiss Halivni, *Midrash, Mishnah, and Gemara: The Jewish Predilection for Justified Law*, Cambridge: Harvard University Press, 1986.
Alistair Kee, *Constantine versus Christ*, London: SCM Press, 1982.
Ramsay MacMullen, *Christianizing the Roman Empire* (A.D. 100–400), New Haven: Yale University Press, 1984.
Jacob Neusner, *Judaism in the Matrix of Christianity*, Philadelphia: Fortress Press, 1986.
———, *Judaism and Christianity in the Age of Constantine*, Chicago: University of Chicago Press, 1987.
Elaine Pagels, *Adam, Eve, and the Serpent*, New York: Random House, 1988.
Rosemary Radford Reuther, "Augustine and Christian Political Theology," *Interpretation* 29 (1975): 252–65.
Jonathan Z. Smith, "To Replace," in *To Take Place: Toward Theory in Ritual*, Chicago: University of Chicago Press (1987): 74–95.
Günter Stemberger, *Juden und Christen im heiligen Land: Palästina unter Konstantin und Theodosius*, Munich: C. H. Beck, 1987.
George Hunston Williams, "Christology and Church-State Relations in the Fourth Century," *Church History* 20:3 (1951):3–33, 20:4 (1951):3–26.

17. Lawful Powers

Sebastian P. Brock and Susan Ashbrook Harvey, *Holy Women of the Syrian Orient*, Berkeley: University of California Press, 1987.
W. H. C. Frend, "The Monks and the Survival of the East Roman Empire in the Fifth Century," *Past and Present* 54 (1972): 3–24.
Timothy E. Gregory, *Vox Populi: Popular Opinion and Violence in the Religious Controversies of the Fifth Century*, Columbus: Ohio State University Press, 1979.
W. Stewart McCullough, *A Short History of Syriac Christianity to the Rise of Islam*, Chico: Scholars Press, 1981.
John Meyendorff, *Imperial Unity and Christian Divisions: The Church 450–680 A.D.*, Crestwood, N.Y.: St. Vladimir's Seminary Press, 1989.
Jacob Neusner, *The Incarnation of God: The Character of Divinity in Formative Judaism*, Philadelphia: Fortress Press, 1988.
———, "Is the God of Judaism Incarnate?" *Religious Studies* 24 (1988): 213–38.
———, *Judaism, Christianity, and Zoroastrianism in Talmudic Babylonia*, New York: University Press of America, 1986.
G. A. Williamson, trans., *Procopius: The Secret History*, London: Penguin Books, 1966.
Dimitri Z. Zaharopoulos, *Theodore of Mopsuestia on the Bible: A Study of his Old Testament Exegesis*, New York: Paulist Press, 1989.

18. Sequel

Harold Berman, *Law and Revolution: The Formation of the Western Legal Tradition*, Cambridge: Harvard University Press, 1983.

G. R. Elton, *Reformation Europe 1517–1559*, London: Collins, 1963.

Judith Herrin, *The Formation of Christendom*, Princeton: Princeton University Press, 1987.

Jacque Le Goff, *Your Money or Your Life: Economy and Religion in the Middle Ages*, Cambridge: MIT Press, 1988.

Lester K. Little, *Religious Poverty and the Profit Economy in Medieval Europe*, Ithaca: Cornell University Press, 1978.

Colin Morris, *The Papal Monarchy: The Western Church from 1050 to 1250*, Oxford: Clarendon Press, 1989.

Paolo Prodi, *The Papal Prince—One Body and Two Souls: The Papal Monarchy in Early Modern Europe*, Cambridge: Cambridge University Press, 1988.

Richard E. Sullivan, *Heirs of the Roman Empire*, Ithaca: Cornell University Press, 1960.

Index